T0214011

Advanced Persistent Training

Take Your Security Awareness
Program to the Next Level

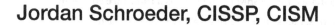

Jordan Schroeder, CISSP, CISM

Apress®

Advanced Persistent Training

Jordan Schroeder
Edinburgh, United Kingdom

ISBN-13 (pbk): 978-1-4842-2834-0   ISBN-13 (electronic): 978-1-4842-2835-7
DOI 10.1007/978-1-4842-2835-7

Library of Congress Control Number: 2017943503

Cover image designed by Freepik

Managing Director: Welmoed Spahr
Editorial Director: Todd Green
Acquisitions Editor: Nikhil Karkal
Development Editor: James Markham
Technical Reviewer: Gandhi Aryavalli
Coordinating Editor: Prachi Mehta
Copy Editor: Kim Wimpsett
Compositor: SPi Global
Indexer: SPi Global
Artist: SPi Global

Distributed to the book trade worldwide by Springer Science+Business Media New York, 233 Spring Street, 6th Floor, New York, NY 10013. Phone 1-800-SPRINGER, fax (201) 348-4505, e-mail orders-ny@springer-sbm.com, or visit www.springeronline.com. Apress Media, LLC is a California LLC and the sole member (owner) is Springer Science + Business Media Finance Inc (SSBM Finance Inc). SSBM Finance Inc is a **Delaware** corporation.

For information on translations, please e-mail rights@apress.com, or visit www.apress.com/rights-permissions.

Apress titles may be purchased in bulk for academic, corporate, or promotional use. eBook versions and licenses are also available for most titles. For more information, reference our Print and eBook Bulk Sales web page at www.apress.com/bulk-sales.

Any source code or other supplementary material referenced by the author in this book is available to readers on GitHub via the book's product page, located at www.apress.com/9781484228340. For more detailed information, please visit www.apress.com/source-code.

Printed on acid-free paper

To my wife and daughter:
Contentment is knowing River ...

Contents at a Glance

Contents

About the Author

Jordan Schroeder is a former department head at a technical school and corporate trainer. As an information security expert and a moderator of the Security.StackExchange.com site, he is dedicated to researching and delivering effective and innovative methods to teach professionals and laypeople alike how to digitally secure their organizations and the assets they control.

Jordan developed and runs SelfPhish, a phishing education and research platform aimed at discovering an individual's vulnerability to different types of social engineering attacks and then tailoring security awareness training to that individual. His experience and research through SelfPhish forms the basis for many of his opinions and recommendations in this book.

About the Technical Reviewer

Aryavalli Sriranga Narasimha Gandhi is a seasoned information security expert. He has been fighting as a soldier for the past 18 years, defending families from cyber-attacks, malware, and APTs (bots) by providing integrated security solutions on-premises and in the cloud and by reviewing security effectiveness at the compute, hyper, network, and app layers. He has represented OWASP as a global leader, driving security awareness across the globe. In addition, he has been a seasoned speaker about information security at NIT, Trichy, step-up conferences, and several nonprofit security conferences.

Acknowledgments

I wish to extend my gratitude to the following people who showed their support throughout this project:

Mark Chapman (PhishLine)
Winn Schwartau (The Security Awareness Company)
Joe Ferrara (Wombat Security Technologies)
Todd Lefkowitz (Rapid7)
Nick Santora (Curricula)
Rohyt Belani (PhishMe)
Chris Hadnagy (Social-Engineer.com)
Geordie Stewart (Risk Intelligence, Ltd.)
Alison Truelove
Richard Evans
Dan Buhler
Secure the Human Community

In addition to the companies that have provided their insights on the topics in this book, the following companies have been wonderful in their support for this project:

www.PhishMe.com

www.Social-Engineer.com

www.TheSecurityAwarenessCompany.com

Foreword

I cannot believe I fell for it!

About a month ago, a semi-authentic-sounding stranger asked me to review a book he was writing on phishing. His unsolicited e-mail was very polite and personalized. It promised to mention my company alongside my competitors, who were already included in the alleged book. It had a link to a somewhat offensive-sounding web site, GoPhishYourself. A few words were consistently misspelled from my U.S.-centric perspective. Of course, there was urgency to "act now before the publication date." If I agreed, he promised to send me a draft of the book as a PDF attachment.

As a "visionary leader" in the field of automated social engineering and security awareness training, it was not possible to ignore such an epic phish! With proper technical controls and a keen sense of irony, I carefully clicked the link, replied to the e-mail, and opened the PDF.

Unbelievably, not only did the draft of the book seem legitimate, it was actually good!

On our first phone call, I had to get to the bottom of what this author, or seriously committed phisher, wanted from me. Surprisingly, he did not want sponsorship money, credit card numbers, or bitcoins. He was an educator, information security professional, trainer, software developer, and blogger who felt that there was a book that needed to be written. To complement his extensive hands-on experience, he had spent a lot of time researching and talking to other educators, security professionals, and leaders in the security awareness industry. He was open to feedback and was committed to sharing his best work with the information security community.

Fast-forward through many in-depth phone calls and several major revisions, and the book is now a reality. The book was written for the growing number of information security professionals and trainers who need to take an established information security awareness program to the next level. After spending many years working with the best people in this profession, I am happy to be invited to make a small contribution to Jordan's work.

For the first part of the book, the style is to provide a full explanation of some fundamental security awareness concepts, with a wealth of specific references for further research and support. About halfway through the book, Jordan's style really shines, with thought-provoking insights and references that are not typically found in this context. Jordan has a way of filling in the gaps for theories or articles that were on the fringes of visibility and taking them front and center. All you need to do is kick back and read a few succinct paragraphs to gain a better understanding of some pretty sophisticated concepts. He then goes a step further to share the voice of other information security awareness leaders. Believe me, it is not easy to get a hold of these people, much less get them to take the time to contribute to a project. I wonder if he phished them too?

The book starts out with an introduction to the challenges faced by information security awareness teams. It is a good warm-up to get us on the same page as Jordan describes many of the common challenges faced by information security professionals charged with running a security awareness program, without the benefit of also being trained educators. Jordan provides some great insights into how to change habits and affect behaviors. As security professionals, we have all experienced the struggle to overcome the challenges to motivate adoption without necessarily being armed with formal concepts such as overcoming "inconvenience without benefit."

The book also talks about building active feedback into a mature program using gamification and habit coaching techniques to improve the effectiveness of the program. I like how Jordan is not afraid to share his perspective with objective references to support the position. The quality bibliographic references will be useful to help growing programs get to the next level.

At this point, Jordan really steps up to provide interesting insights on how to create a partnership with the learner. His real-world experience shines when sharing thoughts on incident response. I looked good in a meeting just the other day because I shared his concept of "report and then get trained" as a possible method to increase the effectiveness of an incident response program.

The coverage of persistent training provides a nice background for training concepts such as graduated learning and spaced repetition. He also shares some useful advice about not getting carried away with your mock phishing tests, which is a common problem because it is just so much fun!

Jordan wraps up his dedicated work by sharing some professional tips that quickly go beyond the obvious. All of us are vaguely aware of generational differences in the workforce, the importance of relating to real attacks, and the value of "train the trainer." Jordan's tips will help you take your program to the next level with confidence.

As a whole, the book provides solid insights into improving your enterprise information security program. It arms the reader with thoughtful views and supporting references to help all organizations improve. The concepts in the book have already helped me sound more educated while igniting or reigniting some lively debates, rants, and discussions with my friend Chris Hadnagy, social engineering guru and author of *Phishing Dark Waters* and other titles.

While part of me is still wondering whether this whole project is the world's most epic phishing scam, we all will undoubtedly learn from the insights and research embedded in the following pages. Jordan's book is a clear benefit to our industry and, indeed, is a book that needed to be written. Enjoy!

Mark T. Chapman, CFE CISM CISSP CRISC
President and founder, PhishLine LLC
Milwaukee, Wisconsin

CHAPTER 1

Challenges Faced by Organizations

Security awareness programs are *wonderful*: managers *wonder* why users fail password audits, awareness trainers *wonder* why they have to constantly remind people not to reuse their passwords for different accounts, and users *wonder* why they have to sit through yet another presentation telling them to craft unique passwords for each account. The information in a typical security awareness program is often well-known, yet organizations still have to deal with the very real risks that result from people not following or understanding the awareness material.

The result can be a general frustration around the whole idea of security awareness. Those who need training most have lost interest, and those who provide training have lost faith that training can deliver a return on investment greater than its cost in time and money. In fact, there are those who have created use cases for abandoning awareness programs altogether as a waste of time, because training will never be 100 percent effective, people being who they are (Dave Aitel, 2012).

How does an organization bridge the gap between people sitting through awareness training multiple times a year and people actually doing what they are trained to do? How does a program transition from raising awareness to fostering secure behaviors, and how does one do it in such a way that inspires passion and excitement?

The answer lies in the heart of the problem: people are human. People have incredible strengths and incredible weaknesses, and awareness trainers need to recognize and devise training strategies that acknowledge both. This book introduces two strategies, which, combined, can take your security awareness program to the next levels of effectiveness, retention, compliance, and maturity.

© Jordan Schroeder 2017
J. Schroeder, *Advanced Persistent Training*, DOI 10.1007/978-1-4842-2835-7_1

■ **Try This**   This book makes no assumptions about what kind of security awareness program you currently have. It is my belief that any program, no matter how good it is, needs to be measured, managed, and matured, just as SANS Securing the Human advocates (SANS, 2015). If you have inherited an out-of-date program written in-house or recently purchased a new, customized, and educationally sound program from a leading vendor, the concepts in this book still apply.

I *am* assuming that you are reading this book because there is at least one area of your awareness program that is not meeting your expectations. Keep that area in mind as you read to see whether you can try some of the things suggested in this book.

Training people is rarely simple and never easy. It is not easy when your students are paying you to teach them, and it is even more difficult when the student is being forced to take training and in the process interrupting the work they are being paid to do. In some organizations, training is seen as a welcome break in a workday routine, as long as it remains entertaining, is not unpleasant, and is not too difficult to comprehend. It is into this milieu that awareness trainers are expected to pass on vital knowledge of an organization's policies and security practices and do this in such a way that gets a positive response from users and also enables them to retain knowledge for more than a few days.

The benefits that come from a truly effective security awareness program are enormous. In September 2015, National Counterintelligence and Security Center Director Bill Evanina said this:

> "91 percent of the breaches we've seen in the last few years have emanated from spear phishing. ... Our adversaries do not need to use sophisticated attacks—it all starts with e-mails."
>
> —Sean Gallagher 2015

This means users should be an organization's number-one security concern. Phishing, by itself, is so effective that it is the primary method used by attackers to gain access to secure networks, protected data, and financial accounts (Tim Greene, 2011). This also means that devising a defense against this devastating, continuous, and persistent threat is imperative, and an effectively trained user is the key to that defense.

■ **Try This**   What about your awareness program? What specific areas would have the greatest impact to your organization if all employees followed their training in that area perfectly? What are the barriers to perfection? Do your users understand and believe that they are the key to a strong defense against threats?

Effective Training Is Difficult

What is stopping a security awareness program from being more effective? From my experience, there are two significant barriers that awareness trainers face.

- Awareness trainers are often not trained educators.

- Users perceive that they are being asked to endure inconvenience without a corresponding benefit.

Awareness trainers typically come from a technical information security background, and it is not common that an information security professional is a trained educator (SANS, 2015; Samantha Manke, 2012). This means that when tasked to develop and implement a security awareness program, the average awareness trainer is at a disadvantage. As knowledgeable and competent as the professional might be in the topics to be covered by the awareness program, that professional will experience challenges when converting that knowledge into effective educational material. There are a couple of ways that awareness trainers can address this challenge: investing in improving their teaching skills and purchasing an awareness program. But, both of these approaches are imperfect.

Improving one's skills in training is a great idea, and those delivering awareness training should seriously consider it, but these skills can be expensive to acquire, and they require time to implement and improve. Most awareness trainers do not have a lot of time to dedicate to improving their training skills (SANS, 2015), so this option is not available to everyone. On the other hand, finding and implementing tactical advice on how to make improvements, such as the ones in this book, can help bridge this gap.

Purchasing a security awareness program from a vendor can be an effective educational option because an organization gets to leverage the collective expertise and resources of a trained team of educators. But vendors experience their own challenges in the form of needing to develop curriculum that will appeal to a wide array of potential customers that might not end up being a good fit for any one organization's culture. Cultural fit can be a significant issue for some organizations, especially if an organization's culture is strong and well-defined. Appendix A contains interviews with prominent security awareness vendors that are experts in designing and delivering training material and that have addressed the issues of cultural fit in their own ways.

The second barrier that awareness trainers face is that users are being asked to work in often inconvenient or unfamiliar ways to satisfy their organization's wants and needs (Ponnurangam Kumaraguru, 2007). Although a user might know, at some level, the reasons for being asked to work in a particular way, they can feel that the risks do not affect them personally and therefore might not be as attentive to the awareness material as they would be to material aimed at protecting them from risks that they care about.

"I have to change my password, again? And it has to include symbols? And I can't write it down on a paper stuck to my monitor? I never have to do things like this at home...."

To better understand this perspective, consider the goal of an awareness program to be changing someone's personal bad habits (not far from the truth, as you will see in a moment). Imagine trying to design an awareness campaign to get people to stop biting their pens at work without making any reference to the potential negative personal effects (e.g., damage to teeth and gums, germ transfer, etc.). If all the user hears is how the organization does not like a behavior and is trying to force them to stop it, there is naturally going to be a lot of resistance ("It's *my* pen, anyway") and low rates of compliance ("I'll just try to remember to stop biting my pen when my manager is watching"). For issues such as phishing or patching standards, the problem is similar in that the user is being asked to consistently act in a way that might be contrary to their normal personal habits (Taylor Armerding, 2015).

Habit is the crucial concept to break past the barriers that prevent a security awareness program from becoming more effective. A focus on changing habits helps an awareness trainer of any experience level reach the next level of effective education, and a focus on changing habits helps a user get past the natural resistance to a new way of doing things (Oliver Rochford, 2012).

Knowledge Is Not Enough

Years ago, I moved into a house where the light switch for the bathroom was outside the bathroom itself, which was very unusual in my experience. I lived there for many years, and by the time I moved out, I think I had a 50 percent success rate of remembering to turn the light on before I entered the bathroom. If at any time you were to ask me where the light switch was, I could tell you in complete detail, but in the moment, when it mattered most, with my mind on other things, I had a random chance to get it right. Why? My habit up to that point in my life (I was in my early 20s) was to close the door with one hand while simultaneously turning on the light with the other. There was no real reason for the habit, but it was so ingrained that even after years of frustration and private embarrassment, my personal "compliance rate" of remembering to turn on the light before I walked in the room was abysmal.

Consider, then, people who have been using Internet accounts for 20 years. It is likely that they have devised methods of remembering their myriad user names and passwords over the years in a way that suits them most conveniently. It is also likely that their methods are not compliant with your organization's password and user account policies. Consider also the habits formed over 20 years in answering e-mails and instant messages. These small habits might be small and insignificant, even to the users themselves, and the users might know full well that those habits are contrary to policy, but in the moment, when it matters most, with their minds on other things, they might have only a random chance to get it right.

Bad habits overriding knowledge and good sense is not a small problem. In 2015, the U.S. Department of Homeland Security CISO, Paul Beckman, said that even though phishing simulation e-mails were obviously fake, some employees, including senior officials, would continually fall for them (Sean Gallagher, 2015). Even after repeated training classes, some deep habits continue to override their knowledge.

▨ **Try This** In the areas of your awareness program where people are failing to comply, is it because of a lack of knowledge or because of noncompliant alternative habits?

The next level for a security awareness program, after the facts and knowledge are covered, is to address those habits. But remember the "pen biting" scenario discussed earlier. It is not enough to simply demand new habits; users need to be motivated and supported to adopt new habits. For technology professionals, technical controls are going to be more familiar than trying to affect the desires of a group. However, it is possible to affect the desires of even a large group, by making tactical changes to the work environment that in turn trigger small adaptations in both attitude and habit among the users. That may sound daunting, but it is entirely possible. To do it, we need to look into human motivation and behavioral modification techniques, which we will delve into in the next chapters.

■ **Try This**   Why would your users want to use their current habits over newer, more secure ones? What wants or needs might the old habit satisfy? What fears might be associated with giving up the old habit? What new wants or needs could you encourage that would replace the existing ones? What could you do to ease any fears of giving up the old habit in order to support the desire of adopting a new habit?

These are big questions, but you should take some time to really dig into them because the answers are fundamentally important to get into the minds of your users. If it is possible in your situation, consider asking some users directly or sending out a survey. The goal is not to correct your users but to listen to them.

CHAPTER 2

■ ■ ■

Active Feedback

There are popular information security catchphrases that attempt to make a comparison between patching systems and patching people (or even patching stupidity). While it is certainly possible to implement strategies, systems, and techniques that can result in sudden changes to people's habits, it is tempting to take the concept too far and see people as systems that can be "fixed" once and for all. But, people do not work that way. Patching software rewrites the underlying code of a system so that the system consistently behaves in a certain way. Getting people to want to change their habits, on the other hand, is a subtle process that works over time, and it is not an exact science.

How do you get people to want to change? In broad terms, people want to change when they want something that a change will bring them. Like the simplified Darwinian model (actually written by Herbert Spencer and not Darwin according to www.nas.org, but I am not going to quibble), "the habits that survive are the ones that get you something you need." With something like a pen-biting habit, that need might simply be comfort, reassurance, or familiarity, but with information security habits, that need might also be directly tied into respect, keeping one's job, or not wanting to look foolish. Your task, then, is to encourage desirable habits by making a direct link between those new habits and something users want or need.

How do you tap into people's deep desires and needs so that you can motivate them to change? One of the most famous researchers in this field is Abraham Maslow, the creator of *Maslow's hierarchy of needs*.

Maslow broke down human motivation into eight different levels of need.

- Physiological

- Safety

- Belonging

- Esteem

- Cognitive (to know/understand)

© Jordan Schroeder 2017
J. Schroeder, *Advanced Persistent Training*, DOI 10.1007/978-1-4842-2835-7_2

- Aesthetic (order, beauty)

- Self-actualization (realize one's potential)

- Self-transcendence (realize someone else's potential)

Maslow suggested that people are highly motivated to meet the needs of the level that they feel is not yet satisfied. He also suggested that the more basic levels of need must be met before one would be motivated to reach, what he called, the growth needs of *self-actualization* and *self-transcendence* (Abraham Maslow, 1998).

Most security awareness programs go only so far as the cognitive or aesthetic (order) levels, and although those levels are required, it is not enough to affect people's habits. A security awareness program needs to make a direct link between teaching new habits and offering new growth potential to the user. In other words, a security awareness program needs to guide the people of the organization through to self-actualization and self-transcendence in order to affect individual habits. This might sound abstract, but it is actually done every minute of every day in a simple way, with people of all walks of life around the world, and you are likely one of those people.

How? Well, would you like to play a game?

Gamification

The term *gamification* suffers from a bad reputation. It is also often not understood. Many people I talk to think that gamification means turning learning or work into a game, and some feel that it trivializes what should be professional activity into a form of entertainment. However, in its essence, gamification is simply the use of game *mechanics* in a nongame setting. It is not about turning something into a game but rather is about the natural attraction people have toward systems that offer self-actualization.

Gamification offers a direct link to self-actualization.

The Game of Work, originally written in 1984 by Charles Coonradt, explains the basic elements required for gamification and systems that offer self-fulfillment (Charles Coonradt, 2012).

- Clearly defined goals

- Scorekeeping and scorecards

- Frequent feedback

- A high degree of personal choice of methods

- Consistent coaching

Imagine, for a moment, that your manager offered all those elements on a daily basis for your job. Imagine a cumulative record of your daily or weekly accomplishments instead of a periodic review of whether you have hit your deliverables. Imagine having the freedom to meet your goals in whatever way you saw fit and getting encouragement and resources to support you in those choices. Imagine your manager being focused on what you *can* accomplish and offering to stretch you into areas where you can accomplish *more* but not punishing you if you cannot stretch that far. Does that sound great to you? It sounds great to a lot of people, and you can use it in your security awareness program to achieve very high rates of engagement and impact.

Despite the true meaning behind *gamification*, the term causes confusion and resistance. In my experience, it is much easier, and more successful, to use the phrase *active feedback* when speaking with management and users. For the purposes of this book, I will continue to use the term *active feedback*, but it is synonymous with gamification.

The five elements of *active feedback* can be a great way to engage people and boost their compliance rates. They act as a blueprint to design a framework that could transition your training from merely passing on knowledge to fostering new habits by providing a chance for self-actualization. By using phishing awareness as an example, I will cover how to implement active feedback in a security awareness program.

Active Feedback Element: Clearly Define the Goal

The goals in active feedback need to be clearly communicated to the users, and the progress toward the goal must be tracked in some way. The things you use to track this progress may be different from the internal metrics that you use to track the success of the security awareness program. Just like all goals, the goals you present to the user need to be S.M.A.R.T. (thank you, Peter Drucker):

- Specific
- Measurable
- Achievable
- Relevant
- Time-bound

PHISHING AWARENESS EXAMPLE

You could set a goal of zero phishing e-mail incidents by users in a month. You could modify it to make it a department-specific goal (e.g., finance has a goal of zero incidents, HR has a goal of no more than five, etc.), or you could adjust the time frame, depending on the environment and how often your organization receives phishing e-mails.

Remember to consider positive *and* negative goals. Having zero phishing incidents is a great goal, but there is a benefit to setting a goal related to the number of phishing e-mails users report to the security department. It might be difficult to devise a goal when you do not have full control over when a user experiences a specific security situation, such as a phishing e-mail, but that is when "persistent training" can be of great help. See Chapter 4 for more on persistent training.

Active Feedback Element: Score Progress Toward the Goal

Since the goal should be S.M.A.R.T., it should already be measurable. The task now is to make sure the metric is clear to the user and the "scorecard" is accessible. There are many ways to do this, but internal web sites tend to be a natural solution for this type of feedback in most organizations. Whichever method you choose, make sure the scores are clear and updated in a timely manner. If possible, provide the previous time period's score as a means to compare performance.

The trick here is to make the score, and the communication of the score, nonpunitive. Bold indications of failure are not helpful, although an indication that the score has crossed a negative threshold can be informative. Likewise, you need to be careful about whether it is possible for users to see other users' scores. While giving users the ability to compare their scores can trigger healthy competition, especially if the score is a group score, be careful that a user is not shamed as a result. *Scores should measure accomplishments, not failures.*

PHISHING AWARENESS EXAMPLE

You could set up a web page on your security awareness site with the scores of each department for the month, along with trend graphs. As an added feature, you could also name the person who reported the most confirmed phishing e-mails in each department.

Active Feedback Element: Provide Frequent Feedback

Users need frequent feedback on whether their actions are having an impact, or else they will lose the connection between their action and the effect of that action on the goal. As you will see in Chapter 3, you also want to make sure you provide that feedback as soon as possible (Kumaraguru et al., 2007).

There are many ways to provide feedback to users about their goal-related actions, including the following:

- Automated responses built into security systems

- Updates to the user's scorecard

- E-mails

- Phone calls

- Face-to-face conversations

Automated systems are capable of providing instant responses to users, which can be useful. However, the personal touch is also an effective way to reinforce habits and to provide an opportunity for the awareness trainer to be available for discussions about security awareness topics one-on-one with users. Try to offer a combination of the two methods, even going so far as following up on an automated method with a personal conversation.

When a user does something that they were trained to do, consider communicating that fact to the department or organization as a whole. The broad spread of the positive feedback will encourage other users to develop the same habits. Make sure you consult with your HR department about how to communicate personal kudos publicly.

When a user does something that has a negative impact on the goal, communicate it using the same channels as for all private feedback. The user needs this feedback, but remember to avoid the appearance of punishment or shame.

Todd Lefkowitz, VP of professional services at Rapid7, had this to say on feedback:

> *"You want to communicate who the top ten employees are to the organization because it is motivating. You do not want to publish the complete list of employee ranking to the organization, because you want to avoid the public shame of someone being further down on the list. On the other hand, you want to communicate to an employee where they stand because no one wants to have a low ranking."*

> ## PHISHING AWARENESS EXAMPLE
>
> You could send out weekly e-mails with an update of the metrics found on the web site. The frequency of the e-mails will depend on how often the scores might change. For each user who reports a real phishing e-mail, you could compose a special template response e-mail celebrating the success.

Active Feedback Element: Habits to Reach the Goal

To apply active feedback effectively, users need to know about the different habits that have a high chance to positively affect the goal, but the choice of habits and when to apply them both need to be up to the user. In the best-case scenario, users should be able to come up with their own habits that will positively affect the goal, although this might not be possible in all situations. A self-generated habit is far more likely to be adopted and used consistently than a habit that is taught to the user.

Consider possible ways that a user could successfully achieve the goal and communicate those options to the users. Some habits will be better than others ("I could simply never open any e-mails!"), but the choices should be made known and left up to the user. Cover the different options again in refresher materials, making sure that the goal is the focus and not the individual habits.

As a bonus, if a user devises a clever habit that you did not expect, communicate it to the organization as a whole. The positive feedback will be positive reinforcement to the clever user, and the rest of the organization will feel like they have more control over the available methods to achieve the goal.

> ## PHISHING AWARENESS EXAMPLE
>
> You could teach users in the security awareness program about checking e-mail headers, hovering over links before clicking, and confirming unusual requests through alternate channels, and then ask the users for their own ideas based on their experiences and knowledge. Do not incorporate all the new suggestions into the standard training materials so that users in the subsequent training sessions have a chance to come up with those same solutions by themselves. Remember that self-generated habits are more likely to be adopted.

Active Feedback Element: Habit Coaching

Video games have tutorials, sports have coaches, and your security awareness program should have its own habit support process. Coaching does not need to be involved, complex, or even a formal process, but it does need to be considered in the active feedback framework. Bear in mind that this coaching is separate from the normal security awareness program material. The goal is to have small, targeted, and relevant help that is aimed at the individual for the purpose of helping them hone their skills in the desired habit. Coaching is to be freely offered, but not forced on users, in case they do not need or want the additional coaching. It is a good idea to have a two-tiered coaching approach, one basic and one more advanced, in order to offer coaching to a wide spectrum of users.

Questions, especially open-ended ones, used as a conversation starter tend to work well. Another effective approach is to open a conversation about what you, yourself, observed in your workday routine that relates to the goal or habit (e.g., a phishing e-mail you received, even if it was a poor phishing attempt). The idea is to start conversations, to draw out users to talk freely about what they are seeing (or not seeing), and to offer personal support. While this is an inefficient approach and it requires coaches who are comfortable with starting conversations and taking time to lend a hand personally, it is a human approach and engages the user in a memorable way. Remember that the goal of active feedback is *self*-actualization: equip the user to equip themselves. One-on-one coaching is a great way to do that.

Another benefit to offering human-based, one-on-one coaching opportunities is that a culture is created of asking questions and offering insights or observations as a normal part of workday life. Consider replacing the general security awareness posters used in a typical organization with this coaching-based approach for a time. The direct and human approach might result in a higher impact.

PHISHING AWARENESS EXAMPLE

When you are interacting with users for other matters, you can bring up a question like, "Have you seen anything interesting when you hovered before clicking today?"

You could develop more advanced questions for more technically proficient users, like, "Have you seen a URL with the 'constant contact' or 'mailchimp' domains in your e-mails? Ever wondered how they work?"

You could switch out these questions every couple of days with new questions.

■ **Try This**   Looking at one of the habit-based problems that you identified earlier, how do you think you could meet the basic elements of active feedback on an individual basis for your users? How would you implement these elements for everyone in your organization, from the office of the CEO to the mail room?

Multiple Habits

How does a trainer foster multiple different habits? Consider choosing one habit at a time (Karen Pryor, 1999) or habits that do not overlap in frequency or common skills. Password policy and phishing avoidance are a good pair to work on at the same time. Passwords tend to change at predictable and longer intervals, while phishing e-mails tend to be unpredictable, and it is possible to receive multiple phishing e-mails in a single day. Credential habits and e-mail habits also do not have overlapping skill sets.

Overloading your users with multiple habits to improve at once will cause confusion and will trigger resistance and disengagement. Take it slowly, and leverage the success of one adopted habit to help adopt a new one, when users are ready for it.

Awards, Rewards, and Recognition

Naturally, if a system is going to have a score, then it should have some kind of prize, right? Yes, but the type and timing of the prize are important aspects of active feedback to consider. Aaron Dignan, in *Game Frame* (Aaron Dignan, 2011), mentions that prizes that are announced before the game starts are treated with less value and perceived as deserved and earned *awards* instead of *rewards* by those who receive them. Earned awards do not affect behaviors with the same impact as unannounced and unpredictable rewards. While you should consider awards for accomplishing goals, you should also consider the unannounced and unpredictable positive feedback during a user's path toward the goal. We will look more closely into why that is in Chapter 3.

In the phishing awareness examples, I have talked about face-to-face kudos and organization-wide e-mails that recognize an individual's efforts. These are the types of unpredictable rewards that can have a big impact. There is no need for these rewards to comprise material goods or things of monetary value. Dignan suggests that praise, earning the right to make a decision, and access to an experience or opportunity can be valued rewards. Popular video games allow players to dress up their game in certain ways for various achievements. The idea is to offer recognition of the user's efforts as a treat, not as a payment.

For security awareness, we should think about awards for adopted habits and goals achieve but about rewards and recognition for the effort along the way. Certificates, trinkets, and trophies would be good awards, as long as you remember that the users are expecting them and will have the attitude of deserving them. Keep the awards small and something the user can use to talk about what the user *did* instead of what the user *got* in return. Recognition, on the other hand, should be more involved and unexpected.

Employee reward and recognition is definitely a topic that you should bring up with your HR department. They might have their own reward and recognition programs, or they might be able to provide valuable guidance.

Gaming the System

Scores, awards, rewards, and recognition can really work to motivate people, and sometimes that lure is too strong. Sometimes users are so focused on the feedback that they do not focus on the habits you hoped they would develop to get that feedback. In these cases, the users try to exploit weaknesses in the system to get the positive feedback they want in the most expedient way possible. This is sometimes called *gaming the system*. While most people think that this is an undesirable situation, it is a great indication that an active feedback system is working as intended. Users may not be developing the habits the trainer desired, but these users *are* developing new habits to achieve a goal, although perhaps not in a way that would increase their compliance with training.

Instead of getting frustrated or punishing these "gamers of the system," recognize their creative efforts and recognize that the active feedback system you implemented is working. The tricky part is to shift the "gamer's" perspective to reaching the goal and developing habits needed to achieve the goal, instead of getting rewards. It is important to properly reward the gamers, even for their shortcut, and then work with them to develop new goals (and even new rewards) that put them on the path of growth you want them to be on. While doing all this, examine the active feedback system to determine where the weaknesses are and fix them, perhaps with the help of the users who found those weaknesses.

It can be tempting to minimize the gamer's efforts as "cheating," but these users are the ones you need to keep engaged with your security awareness program because they have the preexisting mind-set either to be the security champions in your organization or to be the ones most likely to invent ways to circumvent your technical controls. Either way, these gamers should be the ones you want to identify early, and you should keep them involved in the program as much as possible.

As you have seen, to instill new habits in a person, that person needs to *want* to change their existing habits (Darwin/Spencer). To trigger and support the desire to change their habits, you can tie the change to an opportunity to grow (Maslow). An effective and predictable way of providing a person with an opportunity to grow is to use the self-actualizing systems used by sports and games (Coonradt). It might seem complex, but you have seen how it can fit together in actionable and straightforward ways. To understand why it all works and how to reduce the risk of applying these techniques in unproductive ways, in the next chapter you will take a brief look at the underlying forces driving this process: behavioral modification.

CHAPTER 3

■ ■ ■

Behavioral Modification

Just like *gamification*, the term *behavioral modification* can get negative reactions. It can be associated with animal training, and it can be associated with B. F. Skinner (the father of behaviorism), who has the unfortunate and unfounded reputation for having raised his daughter in a so-called Skinner box to perform conditioning experiments. This is entirely untrue, but the urban legend remains. It is also difficult to use the term *behavioral modification* with the people you want to train. Phrases using some variation of "change your behavior" have connotations related to parenting, so it is usually best to avoid those phrases altogether. Something like "changing your habits" is a much easier phrase to use, with fewer negative connotations. However, in this chapter, I will use the term *behavior* so that the wording aligns with the various sources being cited.

One important note about behavioral modification that is often overlooked, when in fact it is considered possible to instill any behavior that the person is physically and mentally capable of doing. Behavioral modification is not manipulation, a trick, or a replacement for traditional knowledge transfer. For a user to be able to adopt new habits, the user needs to be capable and willing (though not necessarily motivated) to adopt new behaviors. That is why behavioral modification is a *partnership* with the learner and not some kind of hypnotic power to be wielded as a weapon.

Shaping, Not Shaming

The word *shaping* is a behavioral science term for working toward a particular behavior by using a series of small steps that are initiated by the learner. In shaping, you set a goal and then let the person experiment with ways to achieve that goal on their own. The trainer offers feedback when the person makes even the smallest action in the direction of the desired behavior. The process is led entirely by the learner, and the trainer's job is solely to provide feedback. Shaping allows a trainer to create new behaviors from scratch without corrections, force, or potential shame, by simply drawing on a person's natural ability to learn (Karen Pryor, 2007).

© Jordan Schroeder 2017
J. Schroeder, *Advanced Persistent Training*, DOI 10.1007/978-1-4842-2835-7_3

In behavioral science, the initial discovery of this technique led to a revolution in how new behaviors are instilled in others. The previous leading theory (called *successive approximation*) was to make small changes in the environment until the learner acquired the required skills to accomplish the desired behavior. Successive approximation is the natural method most of us might use, like slowly raising a basketball hoop to get a new player to develop the skills to get the ball in the basket. This method can work, but it takes time to slowly build and rebuild the necessary habits as the environment changes, and it requires that both trainer and learner set and achieve a series of goals over time.

Shaping, on the other hand, is a much more efficient approach because the goal is never changed (e.g., the hoop stays in one place), so there is no need to develop intermediary habits that are then unlearned, and learners are in control of the learning process from beginning to end while they create their own methods to achieve the goal.

There are two keys to shaping: volunteered behaviors and positive reinforcement.

Volunteered Behaviors

Volunteered behaviors are the behaviors that the user comes up with on their own in the direction of the goal. Instead of lowering the basket to make it easy to get the ball in the hoop, you reward the learner for standing with the ball, trying to think of how to get the ball up to the basket. Every different attempt to get the ball in the hoop is a volunteered behavior, including when the learner asks for suggestions. You support this aspect of shaping in active feedback by offering feedback and habit coaching while the user experiments with their own ways of accomplishing the goal.

In organizations where I have used shaping techniques, it is not unusual for learners to come to me for feedback on various potential behaviors that they have been thinking about. Even these virtual behaviors (virtual, in that they were only ideas) are valuable for modifying behavior. In the previous example, where you devised questions to ask users in regard to new habits, you seek to draw out these virtual behaviors to provide feedback. In my experience, even if the users lie and say that they used a behavior that they did not (in essence, devising a virtual volunteered behavior), providing positive feedback can still have a powerful effect on subsequent real behavior.

Positive Reinforcement

Positive reinforcement is the second key to shaping. I have been talking a lot about different forms of positive reinforcement throughout this book (awards, rewards, recognition, scores, leaderboards, etc.), so there is no need to explain what forms of positive reinforcement are useful or how and when to apply them.

However, when behavior scientists speak of positive reinforcement as being the most effective techniques for behavioral change, they also mean that a trainer needs to avoid *negative* reinforcement techniques, whether the trainer uses them knowingly or unknowingly.

Punishment is a natural response by trainers to undesired behavior, and it tends to be the first (and often only) response a novice trainer uses. Unfortunately, punishment does not work reliably to correct a behavior; it generates insecurity in the learner, and it can create a bad attitude toward the trainer (Karen Pryor, 1999). If insecurity and bad attitudes are created as a result of an awareness program, then it is definitely a bad situation for security personnel. Resist the temptation to engage in punishment, and focus instead on positive reinforcement of the desired behaviors.

The flip side to punishment is negative reinforcement, where something negative is administered to the learner, which is then removed when the learner does something right. Placing restrictions on a user until they start displaying the desired behavior is a form of negative reinforcement. The danger here is that the user learns to cope with the negative reinforcement instead of being encouraged to behave differently.

In addition to the punishments or negative reinforcements that a trainer might design, many unintended things may be perceived as negative reinforcement or as punishment by the user, such as formal reprimands, technical restrictions, grumpy faces on the security personnel, or even needing to submit a security incident for their own failures. These things may be obviously negative, but punishment and negative reinforcers are defined by the receiver, and the trainer might not predict how things will be perceived by the user (Karen Pryor, 2005). Look for signs of things that are being perceived as punishment by your users' reactions and make adjustments, where possible. Sometimes, negative consequences need to happen because of organizational policy, legal requirements, natural consequences of actions, etc., and when negative consequences are necessary, it is important to attempt to frame those negative things not as a result of the user's behavior but as a means of feedback or as consequences that are happening *around* them, not consequences that are happening *to* them. Focus yourself, your incident response team, and the user on the desired behaviors, and reinforce those.

Incident Response and Security Awareness

It is an incident responder's job to be focused on the incident at hand and the potential threats to the organization. Incident response teams are not focused on making sure the user is perceiving incident response procedures as a positive reinforcement, and this could undermine your behavioral modification efforts. Consider including the security awareness team as part of the incident response team. This way the trainers can directly interface with the user to make sure that the user sees incident response in the right frame of mind: a natural consequence and not a negative reinforcement. Focus on the correct behavior the user needs to employ and on providing clear communication on what happened to create the incident. Most users *want* to do the right thing; they just need clear communication about what the right thing is and how to accomplish it. The moment the user sees impending punishment, they become defensive, secretive, and uncooperative. In a security incident, all of those behaviors are counterproductive at best and devastating to the organization at worst. When the user shows relief as a result of their interaction with the incident responders, you know your teams are doing it correctly.

In one program that I designed, management decided that asking users to inspect or analyze suspicious e-mails was too much to ask of the users, and therefore the desired goal would simply be to report all suspicious e-mails to the security team for analysis. I added a requirement that the incident response team perform individual education to the user about what the responder saw in the submitted e-mail, and we worked it out so that the extra time spent by the incident responder was less than two minutes. This one-on-one training at the point of an experienced security event allowed the team to elevate the knowledge of individuals, which resulted in users voluntarily going the extra step to start using the same analysis techniques on the next suspicious e-mail they experienced, while still performing the required behavior of reporting the e-mail. It is these types of volunteered behaviors you want to see and reward in your organization.

There is an added benefit to the approach of "report and then get trained" that you should not miss. The one-on-one education in e-mail analysis was perceived by the users as a *reward* that the user was entrusted with. This reward was also perceived as a recognition of their ability to handle more complex knowledge, which also made them appear as an expert among their peers. Suddenly, some users were submitting suspicious e-mail reports for the sole purpose of getting the additional training on e-mail header analysis. The more that you can trigger situations where users value extra training, the better your organization will be.

■ **Try This**   How did the incident response team respond to the user in recent incidents involving user habits? How did the user respond to the security team's response? What might have been perceived as punishment or negative reinforcers? How could the security team have acted to trigger a more positive response from the user? What are some changes you can implement with your incident response team to trigger a more positive response from users?

"That User"

"But, we have a user who really doesn't get it! No matter what we try, no matter how nice we are, no matter what severity of punishment we threaten, the user does not change at all! They test well one on one, and they seem to understand the policies and guidelines when they are with security personnel, but when they are back at their regular duties, they make the same mistakes again and again. What do we do?"

This can happen when a user tries to put on a good face for others, but they do not believe in or value the goals, controls, or policies put in place by the organization. This situation can arise in users across the entire spectrum of technical expertise and work experience, and it seems to occur in every organization, no matter how small. Frankly, in this situation, you need to get really creative, but according to behavioral modification expert Karen Pryor (2012), there are things to try.

First, really try to see your security awareness program, your controls, and your incident response procedures from that user's perspective. Are there things that are being perceived as punishments or negative reinforcement? Could those things be changed, even for just this one user?

Second, wait. Sometimes, as the user is exposed to the changing habits of the users around them, they might naturally align themselves with the group. This is not a likely scenario for people who are seen as leaders in the group, though, or if the problem has been ongoing for too long and is now deeply ingrained.

Third, find an opposite behavior to the undesired behavior and reward that behavior for that user. You have a special case anyway, so why not create a mini-active feedback program for them? Does a DevOps administrator keep pushing untested code to production? Start keeping metrics on how often they push tested versus untested code and create rewards for pushing more tested code than untested code; then increase the desired ratio over time.

Fourth, ask them for the *un*desired behavior and reward them for it; then never ask for it again. This approach is advanced, and it might work only for some users, but I have personally done this with success. When it works, it works like a charm. Give the user special permission or make a special request for them to perform the problematic behavior that they know they should not do (but they do anyway). When they do it, provide special positive reinforcement (i.e., a hearty public thank-you for their "unique" help). This puts the power of the choice of when to do the undesired behavior into *your* hands, not theirs, and the user might wait to engage in the behavior until you ask for it again in order to get the recognition. It sounds counterintuitive, and even scary, but it can work very well.

Fifth, change the environment to change the motivation. This is similar to implementing technical controls to create a "no choice" scenario, but it is different in that the underlying motivations disappear. Why is the DevOps administrator pushing untested code to production? Perhaps the administrator feels pressure to meet deadlines. If so, shift the administrator's responsibility to push code that has been tested by another party, and shift the focus of the pressure to the testing team. In this situation, it might also be a good idea to examine management's attitude toward deadlines so that users do not feel the threat of punishment if they do not engage in risky behaviors.

From personal experience, I would add a sixth option, which is to examine the situation to see whether certain people are given a "pass" by management to do noncompliant things because they are high-performers, senior employees, or friends with the right people in management. The cure for this situation, unfortunately, is a culture change in the organization. While changing organizational culture at the top is a topic far beyond the scope of this book, the idea is to get management to value their own controls and processes, even if they are inconvenient. No one should get to circumvent policy controls because of who they are, and every time management gives someone permission to circumvent the organization's controls, the harder it will be to increase compliance of the organization as a whole.

■ **Try This**   Remember that behavioral modification does not work as a way to force or trick people into doing something. Sometimes a person simply is not going to follow the rules. If you feel yourself attempting to use the previous techniques as a method of control over a person, step back and remember that behavioral modification is a partnership.

Attackers Use Behavioral Tricks

Even after all this explanation, some people might still be uncomfortable with overtly employing behavior modification techniques in their organization because they think it is a form of manipulation. Consider this, though: social engineers are masters of manipulating people and preying on insecure behaviors, and it is likely that at least one person in your organization will be targeted by one this year. For an organization to fight against these types of attackers, information security trainers need to understand the techniques attackers use and then devise secure habits and behaviors so that users can protect themselves.

Ingrained habits are the easiest for attackers to exploit. A multi-university study conducted in early 2011 found that active Internet users were especially susceptible to phishing attacks because they do not take the time to evaluate every communication they receive (Tim Greene, 2011). This natural sense of urgency contributes to the statistic that half the respondents to phishing e-mails visit the fake web site within an hour of the e-mails being sent (John Leyden, 2010). In a recent simulated phishing attack that I performed for an organization, 5 percent of the target users clicked the obviously fake link within *two minutes* of sending out a mass e-mail. There is a natural sense of urgency to e-mails that can be heightened by tone and subject matter so that users opt not to take the time to evaluate whether the e-mail is real.

Besides urgency, notification of changes in company benefits (Jaikumar Vijayan, 2011), fear, trust, desire, greed, and curiosity (Thanuja Vasudevan, 2010) can all be used to manipulate users successfully. One study found that the imposition of responsibility that appears to come from a higher authority is the biggest human driver, being 28 percent more effective than greed, which was thought to be the most successful manipulation technique (William Jackson, 2011). The authoritative approach is particularly effective in industries that are highly regulated or in companies that normally operate with a strict authoritative hierarchy (Karla Jo Helms, 2011).

Each of these statistics is an example of users not critically thinking about their actions, either mindlessly going through their work routines or letting their emotions override their judgment. One method an organization can use to combat this type of manipulation is to teach and encourage "mindfulness" while performing one's work. We look at mindfulness in Chapter 6. Whatever method you choose, knowing your organization better than the attackers do will help you protect your organization from those who are just a phone call or e-mail away from a social engineering attack.

Active feedback is an effective approach for affecting behavior and habits, and it works well when people are in a situation such as a sport or a game. However, in a sport or game, the user is in a closed system (the playing field, game room, application, etc.), and the conditions are controlled by the physical space or confines of the application. In these situations, the users are willingly giving their attention to the activity and intentionally constrain themselves to the rules of play. But, this is not the case in a user's day-to-day work activity. In the example of phishing training, the "game" is up to an attacker choosing when and if to send a phishing e-mail to the user. If a user experiences a phishing e-mail only once every couple months, there is insufficient opportunity to provide active feedback. Persistent training, the subject of the next chapter, puts *you* back in control of the game.

CHAPTER 4

■ ■ ■

Persistent Training

Persistent training is a process where you train and test users with an ongoing process of simulations and supplemental training material. Simulated phishing, social engineering tests, and requests made through the ticketing system to do something against policy are all forms of tests that can be used for the purposes of persistent training. The goal, of course, is not to see whether users will fail the test but rather to present an opportunity to exercise the users' training and to follow up with supplemental training if users fail.

More than just putting up posters or holding talks or presentations, persistent training is about creating situations where users have to choose how to act and draw upon their training to make the appropriate choice. Sometimes this means acting like a red team to test your users (if your organization has a designated red team, you will want to get their advice and input), and other times, it simply means creating an artificial learning opportunity for users. While these opportunities can be elaborate or simple, the more effective learning opportunities are personalized and tailored to the learning needs of users, are small enough to slip into users' daily activity unnoticed, and are fully automated.

Persistent training should be an ongoing, integrated process in an organization. Instead of a quarterly (or even yearly) event, users should learn to expect a simulation or test at any time because attacks can happen at any time. Scheduled events can be helpful, too, but there are numerous benefits to ongoing training, including improved knowledge retention rates and the opportunity for the awareness trainer to utilize a "graduated learning" approach that I will talk about in this chapter.

Benefits of Persistent Training

The easiest elements of a security awareness program to include in a persistent training approach are those that can be automated through technology. Of those, phishing simulations are the most common. In most of the research presented here, phishing simulation features prominently, but the findings should be encouraging for any testable element of a security awareness program.

J. Schroeder, *Advanced Persistent Training*, DOI 10.1007/978-1-4842-2835-7_4

Security training needs to be ongoing and certainly more than once per year to be effective. In 2011, the company PhishMe reported seeing no improvement in users' ability to detect phishing attempts when the simulations were performed only yearly. Through ongoing simulations, PhishMe saw a reduction of unaware clickers from 58 percent to single-digit percentages after the fourth round. These results are encouraging considering that the rounds of simulation increased in sophistication as they progressed (William Jackson, 2011).

Wombat Security Technologies' product, PhishGuru, was studied by students at Carnegie Mellon University in 2009. In that study, a month-long test was carried out where phishing e-mails were sent to three groups: a control group, a group that was trained only once on how to spot a phishing e-mail, and a group that was trained twice within two weeks. The group that was trained twice saw significant improvements in the ability to spot and to refrain from supplying information to a phishing attack (Ponnurangam Kumaraguru, 2009).

Ongoing training (and even short durations between training) has been clearly shown to be a superior method to affect knowledge retention and to affect the adoption of new behaviors.

An interesting element in both the PhishMe and PhishGuru studies is that the attack simulations took place in users' own e-mail inboxes, and the automated learning system presented instant feedback to users when they acted. Other research has been done on the approach of embedding learning opportunities into users' normal activities. Northrop Grumman Corporation found that the opportunity for users to experience simulated phishing attempts in their inboxes was better for equipping them to identify real phishing attempts later (Nancy Toppel, 2010). In addition, a Carnegie Mellon University study showed that providing feedback to users as quickly as possible when they did click a phishing link resulted in even higher instances of user success (Ponnurangam Kumaraguru, 2007).

These findings highlight the benefits of presenting ongoing persistent training as an embedded exercise, instead of as sessions detached from a user's reality. The findings also show the impact of providing habit support when a user needs it most. Just like in a sport or game, having a coach there to help you succeed when you stumble has an especially powerful impact on being able to achieve the objective the next time an opportunity presents itself.

■ **Try This**   Think about what impact a focus on persistent training could have on the perception of your traditional security awareness training materials, "lunch-and-learns," and short refreshers. Instead of being isolated, disconnected knowledge sessions, they could be presented as ways for users to equip themselves to tackle the simulated attacks the program has in store for them. Since attackers are lined up to test your users, this potential perspective of the awareness program is apropos.

Graduated Learning

In a well-designed persistent training program, you are in control of the two critical elements of learning and reinforcement: steadily increasing the difficulty in graduated steps and timing the tests and reinforcement to maximum effect.

Graduated learning is a process where the learning material is broken up into defined modules of increasing difficulty. Each module is taught and tested on its own as though it is its own learning project, with its own active feedback cycle and training schedule. All year long, users are presented with new material or new levels of the material and tested on their ability to act based on their new knowledge.

Since persistent training is to be happening year-round, and not in seasonal events, you need to create supplemental training material that covers a broader and deeper scope than what you would need for a yearly training session. Although this sounds like a daunting task, creating graduated modules can actually make creating (or adding) materials easier than creating a single yearly lesson. Breaking up the material into modules means that each module, and each training session, becomes smaller and more manageable for the user. Shorter, targeted training is also easier for users to absorb and retain. The modular approach makes it possible to create material that covers an entire topic without needing to present it all at once. Users unlock the next module when they show that they have mastered the current module. The result is comprehensive training material designed to be dispensed in small, manageable chunks that will not bore the users but will make them feel like they are on a path of growth and challenge.

For example, in the SelfPhish research platform, I divided the phishing awareness materials into levels of increasing sophistication, from learning to identify the clumsiest phishing attempts all the way up to being able to interpret and analyze the PHP variables of a GET request. Users are free to advance at their own pace and to go as far as their technical capabilities, or curiosity, will allow. However, having a "next level" available to them entices users to stretch themselves to reach higher goals than they might normally attempt.

■ **Try This**   Is your training material delivered in one large session? What would happen if you broke it up into modules and let users go through them at their own pace?

As you break up or add new material into different modules, having a module that goes far beyond the organization's expectations of its users is important. Using privacy awareness material as an example, you could include a module covering the finer points of the privacy regulations that your organization is subject to at a level that only a privacy officer or your legal department would normally have to know (you could even get those professionals to help write the advanced material). This module of extreme difficulty places a goal just out of reach for most users that encourages all users to try a little harder than they might otherwise. Do not make this module mandatory; in fact, consider not making anything but the lowest-level modules mandatory, but make it available as an "above and beyond the call of duty" target for your users to reach. Even if a few users attempt to complete the module, your organization will benefit from the additional expertise in even those few users.

Why not make all modules mandatory? It is tempting to force all your users through the material that you have put in place, but remember that a core element to active feedback is that users go through the training and habit-forming process at their own pace. Your organization will undoubtedly have a requirement of some level of competence in some material, and it is understandable to make those "bare-minimum" modules mandatory, but you risk losing engagement by forcing users to learn all available modules.

Some material cannot be graduated or broken up into modules, either because the subject is too short or because it does not lend itself to being broken up into levels. In these cases, try to replicate the graduated learning approach by breaking up the modules into themes, or themes of examples. Account management might be a topic that cannot be broken up into graduated modules because password complexity does not change, and the policy of a unique password for each account is not a complex topic. An example of what could be done is to teach and test based on themes. Focus on office application accounts in one module, then cloud services in the next, followed by third-party services. The actual learning content does not change, but the themes and examples do.

Spaced Repetition

It might be counterintuitive, but it is possible to test, reinforce, or review material too frequently. Not only do you not want to annoy the user with simulations and tests, but there is a learning process that benefits from breaks in between tests.

Spaced repetition is a learning concept that can create highly efficient ways of studying material, without reviewing the material too much. The goal of spaced repetition is to review the material just at the point where you are starting to forget it. Having to reach a little to remember something can powerfully ingrain the material into your memory more so than rote repetition. The basic process behind spaced repetition is to increase the time between review periods when the person can successfully remember the material and to decrease the time between review periods when the student is not successful.

In the first forms of spaced repetition using flash cards, students would have multiple boxes in which to store the cards. One box would be reviewed daily, the second box would be reviewed every three days, the third box would be reviewed every five days, and so on. All new cards would start in the first box, and when the student found it easy to recall the answer, they would place the card in the next box. If the student struggled but successfully remembered the card, it would remain in its current box. And, if the student failed to remember the card, the student would place the card in the previous box for more frequent review. If you have not tried this technique for your own study purposes,
I highly recommend you try it, either with physical cards or with one of the many software applications designed for this purpose.

For persistent training, spaced repetition means you can maintain the ongoing nature of the training without annoying a user with an unnecessary frequency. Spaced repetition makes it possible for someone to get extra help on a certain topic by providing increased frequency of review, but those who do not need as much help are not annoyed by training or testing. In all cases, the goal is that each user is presented with a test or a review at the point when they need it most. The consequence of implementing spaced repetition in an awareness program is that the timing of training and tests are completely personalized, instead of scheduled for a department or organization as a whole.

Although there are software applications designed to adapt to an individual's learning needs and craft the optimum spaced repetition period for any topic, this level of detail and control might be a little out of reach for a small security awareness team. The good news is that incorporating a simplified spaced repetition does not need to be technically complex. For instance, in the Carnegie Mellon PhishGuru study, the researchers used a form of spaced repetition by spacing the training and tests in a pattern of two days, five days, and seven days, and then they repeated the cycle. Their intent was to measure the PhishGuru system's ability to increase immediate (two days) and short-term (seven days) retention (Ponnurangam Kumaraguru, 2009). Although the study's purpose was not to test the effectiveness of a spaced repetition algorithm, it does represent one way to approach an ongoing testing schedule.

To implement spaced repetition, you first need to choose the spacing intervals. You will ultimately be experimenting with the intervals based on your organization and how difficult you have made the modules. You could manually designate the spacing or choose a pattern that will make it easier to automate or create a program for. For instance, you could double the time between events, such as 2, 5, 11, 23, 49, and so on.

A pattern that increases the time dramatically if the user always passes a test or review is a good thing. Just remember to put a cap on the maximum interval or you might end up with an interval where the user is never presented with the material ever again. My preference is to cap the interval at three months, but I do not have enough data to justify this decision, other than personal judgment and the ability to say that all users are tested at least quarterly.

Second, after the intervals, you need to decide what to do if the user gets it wrong. You should consider decreasing the time until the next event, but if that is too difficult to manage, at least maintain the current interval. You could try setting a static time period, such as always retraining or retesting three days after a failure, or you could shift the user's schedule down the interval sequence, just like the flash card system. In the case where a user is always failing a module, make sure you have some process for identifying that user and trying a different approach instead of retesting them every day.

As you can probably see, tracking all these schedules for even a small organization can be a challenge. Tools such as spreadsheets, databases, or custom applications can all be used, and I have tried implementing them all. Which method you choose is up to the resources available to you. You could simplify the scheduling by simplifying your spaced repetition approach, but you will lose the personalized touch that individual schedules provide.

There is an added bonus to incorporating personalized spaced repetition scheduling in your security awareness program, which is that users know, without a doubt, that the training is customized to them. That type of personalized attention will make a user feel far more engaged in the materials than with a quarterly training that everyone needs to sit through, especially when the user knows that the timing and frequency of training is entirely up to their ability to succeed. The user will feel more in control, more like it is a game, and more like they are on their own path to growth.

■ **Try This**   How closely can you implement independent spaced repetition for each user in your program? If personalized scheduling were the key to reducing incidents by up to 30 percent, what resources could you obtain to make it possible for each user in your organization to have their own, personalized training schedule?

Integration with Active Feedback

Persistent training directly integrates with the elements of active feedback.

- Clearly define the goal.

- Score progress toward the goal.

- Provide frequent feedback.

- Provide methods (habits) that could be used.

- Support the habit as it takes hold.

With ongoing testing, you inherently define the goal as being able to pass the tests. As long as the tests are clear in their intent, you provide a challenge to be met. Each persistent training event must be tracked so that a user's response, either positive or negative, is recorded and communicated as soon as possible to the user. By providing the test event in the context of the user's normal work activities, you open up the choice of possible responses to the user, which encourages free exploration of methods to approach the test. With an ongoing (perhaps spaced repetition) schedule, you leave it up to users to decide how fast they want to learn or develop new skills or habits. All of these things combine to promote an active feedback approach in a practical way.

A Warning About Persistent Training

There is a fine line between simulating attacks in a safe way to train your users for a real attack and actually attacking your users and being seen as a threat. Remember that your goal is to be a coach and a habit support resource. I have seen security personnel get a little carried away with phishing simulations and unfairly target users or overwhelm users with an onslaught of attacks. Doing so only makes the security personnel the enemy, which is the worst outcome for persistent training because users will not share their struggles with you or seek your guidance on improving.

The entire security awareness program needs to be a safe place to learn, and even a safe place to fail. Persistent training, by its nature, can be something that can make users feel like they are being persecuted or targeted, so it is especially important to make sure you create an environment where users are encouraged, supported, and provided with positive reinforcement, not punishment. It is entirely possible that your users will frustrate you with how often they fail simulations. But, remember to be mindful (see Chapter 6) and to treat persistent training as a process and a path. Listen to your users to identify signs of antagonistic behavior that would defeat the purpose of the exercise. Analyze what in the program might be perceived as a punishment, and seek to resolve it. Above all, it is important to find a way to keep the persistent training program going because the benefits are too important not to pursue.

CHAPTER 5

■ ■ ■

Metrics and Measures

Every security initiative, including awareness programs, should be collecting metrics so that the effect of the program can be understood and the impacts of changes to the program can be tracked. Unlike measuring technical controls, measuring the effects of a security awareness program can be tricky, and as a result, few trainers track the long-term effectiveness of their awareness programs (Ponemon, 2014). According to a 2014 Ponemon study, the most common methods organizations use to track training impact is to measure the user's knowledge right after training or to run user satisfaction surveys. While these metrics can be useful and easy to collect and measure over time, there are many other metrics that could also be considered. Unfortunately, not all metrics can be objectively measured, and the leaders of each organization need to determine which metrics will be informative for them in their unique situation. This makes defining and collecting metrics a mix of art and science. Despite the subjective nature of the problem, there are methods of gathering useful metrics that your organization can use to track the ongoing effectiveness of your security awareness program.

Just like any metrics project, you first need to define the context. Start by defining what *effectiveness* means for your security awareness program. For many organizations, the underlying goal is a reduction in noncompliance incidents and the elimination of data breaches, but that is a general intent behind security awareness programs, not necessarily a specific, measurable, attainable, relevant, and time-bound (S.M.A.R.T.) goal of the program itself. Many security awareness programs are put in place by an organization to address particular risks. If that is true in your organization, work to tie the metrics you define to the specific risks that are of concern in your organization. Doing so will make it much easier to show management the direct return on investment (ROI) of the program and any changes you make.

Do not go any further in defining metrics until you have a clear understanding of how the metrics fit in with the goals of the program and with the organization's goals. Each module, each learning topic, and each piece of security awareness material has its own goal and, hence, its own metric for effectiveness. But, do not try to define the effectiveness of all those elements right at the start or you will risk getting overwhelmed. Start with the program as a whole, and then as you implement new material or update existing material, define what effect that material is intended to have.

■ **Try This**   Do you have S.M.A.R.T. goals for your awareness program for one-year and five-year time frames? Are you defining S.M.A.R.T. goals for each new training initiative or module?

Once you have defined what effectiveness means by defining the specific, relevant goals of the program, look for the specific, relevant metrics that will help inform you about the progress toward that goal. For instance, is the goal to increase knowledge? In that case, measure successful knowledge transfer after training and then later to ensure the knowledge has been retained. Is the goal to change behavior? In that case, define what the behavior looks like, and put monitoring in place to watch for and measure that behavior. Each activity of the security awareness program needs to be designed to help the users and the organization work toward these goals, and each activity needs its own set of metrics to track its progress toward the larger goal. You will find many examples of specific objective and subjective metrics later in this chapter.

An often missed part of defining metrics is to look at the opposite side of the metric to define the barriers and influences that might exist to hinder the intended effect. For example, if you are measuring how often untested code is released into production, the things that might influence this situation are unrealistic deadlines or pressure from management. Once you define an effect and how to measure it, these barriers and influences will be a lot easier to identify. Some of those things themselves can be measured, and you can include them as metrics to track. This is particularly true when you want to measure behavioral change.

Finding the right balance of having enough metrics and not having too many can be a puzzle. Gathering data on every aspect of every learning initiative is neither helpful nor necessary. Once you have properly defined what the metrics of an effective program are, you can focus your data collection around those areas. On the other hand, not having enough data can result in misleading conclusions, if you do not have context.

Context for metrics can be more important than people realize. Make sure you understand the issues around each metric for your organization. Because you are training people, not programming machines, subtle things such as the effect of recent news on people's behavior, as well as big things such as cultural issues or a new organizational policy, can affect metrics. Because of this, it can be helpful to review the program's metrics on a frequent basis to make sure that the results are interpreted in the context in which they were collected. You can then amend the reporting of the metrics with your interpretations and relevant context.

Once you have a set of metrics that will help you figure out how well your security awareness program is doing, keep looking for new metrics to enhance your understanding. Ask what other organizations use to track effectiveness and see whether those data points might work within your organization. Also, consider a third-party perspective and get an external auditor to look at your program and suggest improvements. Auditors are run on metrics, and they tend to know what metrics will be beneficial. Audits are a little like going to the doctor for a checkup: you might feel fine, but the doctor has a different set of metrics that might uncover something that needs to be addressed.

Above all, whatever metrics you use or add, it is important to respond appropriately when the data comes in. You might be faced with data that suggests that your recent initiative just did not work, or maybe your whole security awareness program is not returning the results you hoped for. Do not panic, and do not make sweeping changes right away. Like any other ongoing process, the training/progress/metric process is a cycle. Reevaluate the training based on the metrics to see whether the progress is on track, and make changes or additions, if necessary. These new things need to have a defined effect with their own set of metrics. Even though you may have put in a lot of work and effort to get a training project off the ground, do not be afraid to put a subproject or the entire security awareness program itself in review, if it comes to that. Finding the right fit and the right approach for your organization can be a learning process for everyone involved.

Objective Metrics

Objective metrics tend to be easier to gather, easier to interpret, and easier to include in reports to management. They can also be generated through automatic processes. The following are examples of classic objective metrics that you can gather:

- Knowledge tests before, after, and long after training

- Reduction of noncompliance incidents

- Failure during an attack simulation (phishing, etc.)

- User surveys

- Number of users trained

You can gather other types of metrics, too, such as tracking the number of times users comply with training. This will require that the compliant action is something that can be tracked, such as reporting to the help desk, but if your security awareness program is designed to trigger behavioral change, remember to work in metrics to track the successes as well as the failures.

Speaking of the help desk, knowing the help-desk statistics on how many security-related calls come in, how many are false positives, and how quickly the user reported the problem are all good metrics to track as part of an awareness program. Personally, I love the "false positive" metric for the security awareness programs I run, and I want to see a general low level of false positives from all departments, with a spike right after training. If people are reporting false positive security issues, it means they are thinking about security and being proactive about it. Also, with a spike after training, I know that the training has caused the users to ask more questions about their daily work routines and to be more aware. I gauge how effective a training session was by the spike in false positives. If a training session did not result in a spike in false positives the following week, I know something went wrong in that training, somewhere.

As a side note to my desire to see false positives, this type of metric helped me to see that awareness training is much more effective if delivered early in the week. I noticed that people would almost never send in false positive reports in the following week if training occurred on a Friday. Weekends kill the retention of knowledge, and users are much less aware of security issues on a Monday, regardless of how well they were trained a few days before. In my programs, I do not bother with in-person training past Wednesdays.

If you offer voluntary training in conjunction with mandatory training, knowing the trends of the number of attendees is a great way to gauge the general desire of your organization to value security and of individuals to improve themselves. The same is true for the hits on your internal security information site. The visitor trends on your internal site can let you know just how much your users want access to supplementary awareness material and how much value your internal site is providing.

As a trainer, one of the nontraditional metrics I track when I am teaching in a lecture style is the number of questions I get during training. This metric is so important to me personally that I will intentionally create inconsistencies, or purposely fail to fully explain an interesting topic, to elicit questions from the learners. Why? By creating a gap in the information, the students' brains switch from being passive consumers of the information to being active learning participants, and I find that they internalize the material to a much greater degree. If I have these gaps in my presentation and the students do *not* ask questions, then I know the session was probably ineffective, and the entire group likely needs supplemental training. This type of metric is a manufactured metric, with specific triggering conditions and specific interpretations, but it shows you the types of metrics to look for and how your security awareness program can be modified to track the things that are relevant to you.

Remember that no one metric will tell you what you need to know. The collection of a variety of metrics will give you a much clearer picture of your program and your organization's security posture as a whole.

Subjective Metrics

Subjective metrics are harder to define, and by their nature, they will depend on the person or people gathering them. This is definitely the realm of "managing by walking around," either physically or virtually. Using your gut or your intuition will tell you a lot about your program, but even though the data is subjective, take the time to *write it down* and track it over time. If it helps, create a survey for yourself and your team to capture your collective instincts on the effectiveness of your program.

Here are some subjective questions you can ask of yourself and your team:

- Is the security team seen as a credible and helpful resource for help and support?

- What is management's attitude toward the program?

- What offhand comments are made about training, the policies and procedures, and the security team?

- Is there a management focus on meeting compliance or a focus on changing the culture?

One of the other aspects of your security awareness program that you can track is its effectiveness on your organization's culture. If you want to survey your users to get a handle on the culture, then you tend to need to approach the questions from a different angle than asking direct questions. Ask about the impacts of the culture instead of the culture itself. Ask questions such as these:

- Who would you talk to if a security event occurred?

- Do you feel that you can report an incident without fear of retaliation?

- Do you feel pressure to go against policy?

- Are the top performers in the organization allowed to go against policy to get their jobs done?

These types of questions will help to shine a light into the security culture of your organization and might expose issues that could be undermining your security awareness efforts and preventing your program from becoming more effective.

CHAPTER 6

Pro Tips

The workforce demographics in the West are rapidly changing, and those changes will impact how security personnel and awareness trainers need to communicate with users.

The Millennial Factor

With the Baby Boomers and the Gen Xers moving toward retirement, Millennials are about to become the largest generation in the workforce within the next ten years (Richard Fry, 2015). With this younger generation comes a radically different view of technology, different values in regard to privacy and ethics, and different expectations of their responsibility to act securely.

One of the surprising outcomes of a Carnegie Mellon PhishGuru study was that those aged 18 to 25 were more likely to click, and give information to, a phishing site than any other group in the study, even after training (Ponnurangam Kumaraguru, 2009). While the older demographic groups behaved more securely from the start, the youngest group remained the least secure throughout the study. In phishing simulations that I have carried out, Millennials have been the ones who were the fastest to click phishing links, sometimes clicking links before they even had time to read the content of the e-mail.

From a generational perspective, a Millennial is generally defined as someone born between 1980 and 2000. These people were teenagers when the Internet exploded onto society or cannot remember a time without the pervasive reach of a global communications network and digital media. Growing up in an information-based society appears to have affected how Millennials perceive information. According to studies (Taylor Armerding, 2015), Millennials value open, instant, and convenient communication that enables them to be productive, and they will find ways to work around any measures set in place to protect that communication channel if those measures are inconvenient (including restrictive organizational controls and policies). Even if Millennial workers follow policy and maintain

© Jordan Schroeder 2017
J. Schroeder, *Advanced Persistent Training*, DOI 10.1007/978-1-4842-2835-7_6

technical controls at work, it is not likely that they will follow the same secure measures at home. This makes it possible for a hacker to gain access to a user's personal device and use that as a launchpad when the user brings their own device into the office (which they will most certainly do).

Knowing the challenges of the Millennial mind-set and how to address those differences in your security awareness program can be helpful (Steve Corbett, 2008).

- Millennials tend to expect certain qualities in a training program for it to be engaging. Production values are a factor, and anything that looks unintentionally "cheesy" or is not sleek and efficient in design will have trouble engaging Millennials.

- Short and on-demand training modules will help this group to connect to the material (this microlearning approach is in line with the persistent training and graduated learning approaches of this book).

- The more interactive the training material is and the higher levels there are of personal connection with the instructor, the better the training experience will resonate with this audience.

Take a look at your existing training materials and see where these qualities can be increased. How does your material look? Does it look cluttered and dense with information? Work with your marketing, art, or design department to find ways to make it cleaner. Are you trying too hard to seem "young" in your materials? Authenticity is a value for Millennials, in general, so look at ways to change the tone of the material to sound more like a person talking to another person over coffee. You'll learn more about copywriting techniques later in this chapter. Would you characterize your material as a novel or a brochure? Consider breaking up materials into smaller units to be delivered over a longer time frame. Although it is good advice for every awareness professional, make a special effort to be more accessible on social media, at company social events, and wherever else this demographic chooses to make a community. These small changes can have a big impact with this important and growing demographic.

This is not to say that all your materials need to cater solely to one demographic. Figure 6-1, from the research of Corbett (2008), can help you optimize your training approaches to reach the different generational learning styles in your organization.

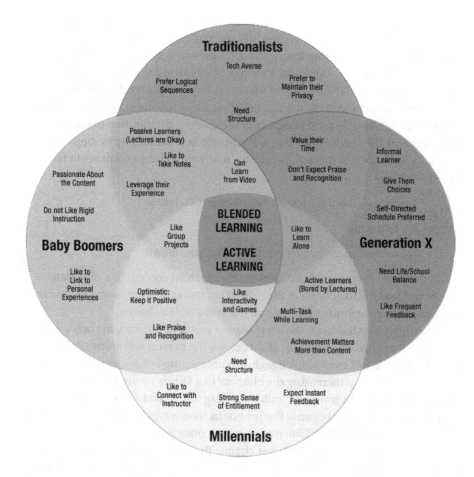

Figure 6-1. *Targeting different generations from the encyclopedia of educational technology*

How Near-Miss Bias Affects Security Awareness Training

Near-miss bias is a cognitive bias that negatively affects people making risk-based decisions. When people have access to data about how often a failure *almost* happened (near-misses), they tend to wrongly overvalue that data over all other types of data, including calculated probabilities, or even data on how other organizations or people have been affected. When they see that they have experienced multiple near-misses, they begin to perceive themselves as lucky, and this irrational feeling can override more sensible behaviors.

This is the same effect that can be seen in the phenomenon of declaring "winning streaks" in sports or games. The wins in these runs of good luck are seen as somehow linked together, and each new win is seen as proof that the successes will continue. But, in fact, streaks of this kind are normal and frequent in any activity, even if the chance of success is low. People tend to link the success events because such streaks defy their expectations of how probability should play out. People tend to expect to see an even distribution of successes and failures as they experience them. For example, if something is supposed to have a 50/50 chance of success, people naturally expect the outcomes to fall in an order such as the following:

success, failure, success, failure, success, failure

and not the following:

success, success, success, failure, failure, failure

In the latter example, after experiencing the third success in a row, most people will rate the likelihood of the next event being another success as quite high, even if they technically know that it is still a 50/50 chance.

Near-miss bias has been shown to skew a person's thinking in such a way that when there has been a string of successes, the person will engage in riskier behavior. People will even stop engaging in preexisting behaviors that mitigate risks and thus end up increasing the chances of a failure event. For instance, a person might have a complete understanding that downloading programs from illegal sites is risky because the programs have a high chance of being infected with malware. But if the person tries it once and does not experience an infection, then there is a much higher chance they will try it again. In fact, if they download programs a few times without experiencing infections, they will start to believe that their previous understanding of the probability of infection does not apply to them. Maybe they found a download source with a much lower rate of infection, or maybe the types of programs they are downloading are infection-free. The person will hold on to these beliefs strongly and will dismiss the suggestion that the files were, in fact, infected but that their antivirus program simply did not detect the infections. More than that, they might go so far as to stop updating or maintaining their antivirus software because "they don't need it." Perhaps you have personally seen a scenario like this.

This can create a problem for awareness trainers who are trying to impress upon their users the importance of engaging in established risk mitigation behaviors or adopting new secure habits. It is not that users do not believe the facts that trainers present to them but rather that the users alter their perception of the facts based on their recent experience of a string of near-misses.

"I know that there is a high chance that I could get infected by downloading this file, but I've been OK so far...."

To combat this way of thinking, focus on two main things in your training: the probabilities surrounding the risk of danger and just how lucky the users are that they have not yet experienced a problem. When people are told the calculated probabilities and that there is a disaster waiting to happen, people tend to stop seeing the past successes as being linked, and therefore the idea of a "streak" is minimized. For instance, show users how quickly a weak password can be cracked and how often automated scanners try to brute force into accounts in your organization. The message should be, "It's just a matter of time." Hold to this message even when users, managers, or senior executives dismiss you and they will eventually start to see the issue in a new light.

Near-miss bias is a big topic, and it has far-reaching impacts for security personnel. For further research into the topic of near-miss bias in decision-making, refer to the following:

- "How Near-Misses Influence Decision Making Under Risk: A Missed Opportunity for Learning" at `http://www18.georgetown.edu/data/people/tinsleyc/publication-40246.pdf`

- "How Near-Miss Events Amplify or Attenuate Risky Decision Making" at `http://create.usc.edu/sites/default/files/publications/hownear-misseventsamplifyorattenuateriskydecisionmaking_0.pdf`

Lie

Sometimes the best way to get to the truth is through a lie.

Early in my teaching career, a mentor provided me with what I consider to be the best advice of my teaching career: lie. If a student is having trouble understanding a concept using standard methods, tell them a lie that they *will* accept that resembles the truth. Then, once they have accepted something that is similar to the truth and internalized it, it is easier to correct the lie with reality.

I thought my mentor was nuts. At first. When I tried it with a student who was blocked on a concept, it worked so well that it changed me as an educator. The point my mentor was trying to show me was that teaching is not about focusing on the truth of the material but about focusing on the mind of the student. Figure out what the student *will* accept and use that as a first step on a path to deeper understanding.

A security awareness professional who I spoke to has also seen this work well not only with her students but with herself. She says, "We used to call it reverse psychology in the 1960s." She likens the approach to the established teaching method of "moving from the familiar to the unfamiliar—if you can state something in terms the learner knows well, they are much more receptive to adaptation."

Lying as a springboard to the truth can work well in security awareness when used with students who are not technically proficient. If you need a student to accept technical details to move forward with training but the student is resisting, you can figure out how the technical details are being perceived and work with them (no matter how fictitious those details might be). Once the student is past their barrier and successfully learning, you can go back and correct the details using the student's new perspective.

For example, imagine that a particular user is having trouble understanding the need for special characters in their password, and they are starting to get stubborn about the issue. While the truth of the matter has to do with the number of bits of entropy that the added characters provide, that fact is never something that you will talk about with the user. You could provide a mild generalization and tell the user that the special characters make it harder to guess the password, but they may come back saying that they could just very well devise a long, all-lowercase passphrase that is easy for them to remember and that this ought to be difficult for an attacker to guess. In this case, you might benefit from a gentle lie: "Yes, you could create a long passphrase, but all the words in it can be found in the dictionary. It is too hard for attackers to include special characters while trying to guess all the dictionary words, so they tend not to use them. By adding special characters, you beat their dictionary attacks." Although this is *almost* true in practice and although it focuses only on a dictionary attack method and not a brute-force character method, it might help the user get past their initial barriers. After they accept this small lie, you can correct it later by explaining how special characters greatly increase the work an attacker needs to do to guess a password.

There are two obvious traps to avoid: lies too strange to correct and feelings of betrayal. In my experience, these are not common issues but are still issues to watch out for. To prevent lies that are too strange, use the smallest lie possible, given the extent of the user's understanding. Imagine a user who still does not understand the special character requirement for passwords and the "attacker" concept is too confusing for them. In the past, I might have said something like, "The computer needs your passwords to be complete sentences with proper punctuation." Although this lie is extremely useful, it is a lie that is too difficult to correct when the user learns that it is not true or if your organization has a system with a low maximum character count limitation that will not allow for full sentences. For students who might end up feeling betrayed, you will have to manage the trust relationship and come to a mutual understanding. Keeping your lies as small as possible will help, as will making it clear that the purpose of the lie was to help the user understand the material and not to deceive.

Despite the potential pitfalls of lying, my mentor's lesson stands firm: focus on the mind of your student and you will not stray far from success.

Customize

Customize awareness material as closely as you can to the department, role, or person.

A 2014 Ponemon Research Institute and Security Innovation study (Ponemon, 2014) included a startling fact: few respondents said that they customized their awareness materials to the finance department (only 10 percent did), but many did customize material for the IT department (66 percent). This is a large, overlooked area of potential gains in a program's effectiveness.

Customizing the material to the audience, even to the person, has a huge impact on attentiveness during training and retention afterward. Every example in training should be customized as much as possible. For example, showing an HR phishing e-mail to the members of the shipping department forces the students not only to try to understand the technical and conceptual points you want them to absorb but also to extrapolate the actual content of the e-mail to their own experience. It can feel like being trained on how HR should respond to phishing e-mails, instead of how they themselves should respond. Showing the shipping department a shipping department phishing e-mail lowers the barrier to identifying with the situation and therefore to understanding it.

Awareness materials should go beyond the department level and be customized to the person. This might be feasible only if you are using computer-based training systems that allow this, but in my experience with the SelfPhish research platform, if the examples use the actual name of the student (instead of John/Jane Doe, for example), attention and retention reach even higher levels.

Lots of customization can be a lot of work, but there are ways to cheat a little. When showing phishing samples, for example, you could use company-wide e-mails or something that might be common to all departments and people. For physical and personal behaviors, you can use a person, role, or department that everyone regularly interacts with, such as reception or the IT help desk, to provide a common experience to leverage.

The Home Front

The same security battles fought at work are also waged in the users' homes.

An organization's security awareness program tends to be focused on the policies and guidelines put in place by that organization. The result is that the material can tend to be dry, and the impact on the individual can be lost, which can translate to low compliance. The person does not feel personally at risk, so there is little sense of urgency.

In one organization I worked with, I started "lunch-and-learns" to exclusively teach tips on how users could secure themselves and their families, without mentioning office policies. The material covered recent security news, tips on teaching secure computing for kids, how to maximize the security of personal web accounts, and exciting stories of hackers and their methods that I collected from my work with honeypots. All of the material was focused on personal computing security, and all of it was driven by the questions and concerns of the participants.

The results were surprising. Even though attendance was not required, attendance was high, with high rates of returning attendees. I also found that attendees would reference the material from these sessions when I later supported them in security incidents. In addition, I found that many of the attendees had deeply internalized the technical concepts to the point where they naturally applied in their work what they had learned in the lunch-and-learns.

While it is our goal to get our users to learn and internalize the official material that we are teaching them, sometimes it helps to teach them to secure *themselves* before they will be a partner in securing their organization.

Show Real Attacks

Show an example of a real attack, on a manager preferably, in your awareness materials.

To add punch and relevance to the general knowledge and theory of your security awareness material, show your users an actual recent example of an attack that a manager or other high-level member of your organization had to deal with. Follow it up with personal statements from that manager about what they thought, felt, and did during the event. If such an example is not available from a manager, find another person in the organization who ought to know how to handle the situation, such as an information security specialist or someone who represents a high-value target or has some authority in the organization. Doing this has four big benefits.

- It breaks through the theory/reality barrier and makes the message feel deeply relevant.

- It shows that management takes the material seriously, too.

- Everyone gets to see that management deals with the same issues and is as personally affected as everyone else.

- It is a story.

I once used this strategy while presenting a phishing awareness session to a local company. As I switched slides from one that talked about a generic example of a phishing e-mail to a real spearphishing attempt that the CEO had had to personally deal with, I was amazed by the sudden energy in the room as nearly 100 people sat bolt upright in their seats and focused on the slide. The value of this tip cannot be overstated, and you should find ways to inject these types of examples in as many of your materials as you can.

Copywriting

Copywriting is a marketing skill that is all about getting the reader to take action. It is not about education or even getting the reader to agree with something; it is about action. This is the type of writing that is especially useful for supplemental security awareness material provided between educational sessions, such as posters, banners, or pop-up screens. Every security awareness professional I have met struggles with how to communicate and reach their users in an effective way, and copywriting is one solution to that problem.

When I started looking at copywriting as a way to improve my awareness materials, there were many writing techniques that were immediately applicable within my organization.

- Writing in short digestible chunks

- Using a personal tone to connect with the reader

- Using real-life stories to provide context to the writing

It is tempting to try to cover all of the material for a topic all at once, but that can backfire. By splitting up the material into bite-sized portions, as suggested in Chapter 4, the reader is more likely to complete the material. A personal tone is good for connecting with the reader, so try writing like you would to a friend or a family member. Deepen the connection further by using real-life stories as often as you can. People like to hear stories, and they are more likely to read longer material if it is in the form of a personal anecdote. Stories will also help you to craft a more personal tone.

I used the techniques I learned in copywriting while writing this very book. If you noticed, the first half of the book is in a long format with a lot of theory and links to research. The second half breaks up a large number of topics into short actionable tips and ideas to think about. The second half is also a lot more personal in tone. The first half reads like an organizational policy training program, with every idea fleshed out in full, while the second half reads more like the security posters, tent cards, and brochures used between formal training sessions. What is your response to the two halves of this book? What has engaged you more? What can you take away from the writing choices I made that you could try in your own materials?

To learn more about copywriting, Neville Medhora, from Kopywriting Kourse, recommends the classic book *The Adweek Copywriting Handbook* as a great book for beginners. It is a book about advertising copy, but the ideas are just as relevant to awareness material.

Mindfulness

Besides the benefits mindfulness has on physical and mental health, relationships, and even pain management, mindfulness can be an effective approach toward helping a user maintain secure habits and behaviors at work. It is also an effective way to combat social engineering attacks that seek to trigger and control heightened emotions.

The following is according to www.mindful.org:

> *Mindfulness is a state of active, open attention on the present. When you're mindful, you observe your thoughts and feelings from a distance, without judging them as good or bad.*

From this external perspective users can view their own motivations, understand the context of their actions, and be able to remember their training from the security awareness program.

The following are the nine essential qualities of mindfulness (Melanie Greenberg, 2012):

- Focusing on the present moment

- Being fully present

- Openness to experience

- Nonjudgment

- Acceptance of things as they are

- Connection

- Nonattachment

- Peace and equanimity

- Compassion

How can a security awareness program incorporate mindfulness? Perhaps the most obvious way is to tap into your organization's HR department and jointly promote the ideas of mindfulness in general to all users. From there, the program can reiterate some mindfulness qualities in the context of working securely. Qualities such as being fully present can help a user remember their training when it comes to a particular context. Nonjudgment can help a user not feel so pressured or fearful when faced with a tricky security situation and to feel free to report incidents when they arise.

As a security professional, it is also useful to practice mindfulness when interacting with your users. Nonjudgment and compassion are crucial in making sure that you are working with your users and not against them. You know "that one" user? Try a mindfulness approach and see how the user responds. You might be surprised.

Each One Teach One

What do you do when a learner plateaus? Change their path.

A user can plateau because they have successfully gone through all the learning modules or because they lose momentum partway through, either because of a lack of engagement or because the material has become too difficult for their skill level. When this happens, the user changes from being an active learner to being a passive reactor.

One way to break this plateau is to get the user to teach other users. Bring these plateaued users into the security awareness team to show new users how they approached the challenges. Ask these users to work with you to review changes to the material to make it fresh and more relevant to the organization. Although the added help is useful, the big benefit to getting your users to switch to a teaching mind-set is that it greatly heightens the user's engagement and compliance with the material.

In World War II, Kurt Lewin, a founder of the field of social psychology, was engaged by the U.S. National Research Council to devise a way to get more Americans to eat organ meats because the choice cuts of meat were being sent to the armed forces. Before Lewin started, expert lectures had been presented to the public explaining the underlying reasons for the shortages and extolling the great nutritional benefits of switching to "variety" meats. In addition, expert chefs had been asked to provide recipes and educate the public on how to prepare these new foods. But these efforts were not very effective. Lewin, though, took a different approach. Instead of addressing the public at large, he had a small group of people learn from the experts, and then he did what no one had done before: Lewin asked them to brainstorm ways to help other people understand and follow the recommendations. This had a surprising effect. The people who came up with ways to help other people learn were *far* more likely to follow the recommendations than any other group. The process of coming up with a way to convince someone else to follow the recommendations resulted in greater compliance in the teachers! Lewin's advice to the U.S. National Research Council was to send people out to the community to hold workshops where, at the end, the people brainstormed techniques to teach others and created posters, recipes, and other crafts that the attendees could use to raise awareness (NRC, 1943). The goal was not to make those attendees effective in teaching others but rather to increase compliance in the attendees.

So, by inviting your plateauing users to be potential teachers or partners in training, not only might you find ways to improve your material, but you will also help those users reach increased compliance with the material in an engaging way.

The Attacker's Mind-Set

When a learner is technically competent and needs a new challenge, put them on the red team.

This tip is advanced, and it requires serious planning and oversight to ensure safety, but it can be a great way to keep users engaged and raise the organization's threat awareness.

Just like the "Each One Teach One" tip, this idea puts the user in an active role, but instead of teaching other users, the user is placed in a position of crafting attacks themselves. Making the switch from responding to threats to actually becoming a threat will help the user deeply internalize the impact of potential threats. If you have ever taken a red team course or learned how to use an attack tool, you probably became paranoid of potential threats and saw your normal daily activities in a new light. If a user is ready for it, give them the same opportunity.

Work with users to create attack scenarios and methods to identify and leverage weaknesses in your own organization. You might be surprised with the problems this exercise exposes. If possible, teach the users the tools to carry out attacks and consider working with them to carry out the attack simulations. Nothing will create a security champion in your organization quite like a nonsecurity person being trusted to attack their co-workers.

Obviously, you need to think ahead and work out the consequences if a user is more successful in an attack than intended. Attacks on the finance or HR department, for instance, are generally not a good idea because of the potential for sensitive data being released into an unauthorized user's hands. Attacks within a department, where users will gain access to information that they are already authorized to access, could be the wisest option. You also need to supervise the users to make sure that boundaries of proper etiquette or professional behavior are not crossed.

If you do not want to go so far as to carry out an attack, consider offering a more general training program on attack tools and methods where users are confined to a lab. There are many training resources and free tools available, including the Metasploit Framework and the Metasploitable virtual machine, and many other free, open source tools and safe targets to practice on. For motivated individuals, I highly suggest going so far as to supporting the users in obtaining official certification in the tools, where possible, or attaining more generalized security certifications, even if information security is not their job. A manual laborer who attains a "hacker" certification, and who did so with the assistance of the organization, will be an ardent champion for security and a subject expert in their own department.

Despite the potential pitfalls, keep this tactic in your toolbox of tricks so that your security awareness program can stay fresh and engaging.

CHAPTER 7

Security Culture

Up to this point, we have been looking at the best ways to support individuals in learning how to secure themselves and their organizations using proven education techniques applied at scale. But how does a security awareness professional tackle the challenge of changing how the organization values security awareness? What happens when the organization is happy to learn and do what you teach them, but only at a bare minimum? How do you get the people in your organization to actually care about security?

No matter how up to date your material is or how effective it is at covering the topics that you need to teach, no material will ever be enough to cover all possibilities. At some point, people need to be willing to recognize and adapt to changes in the threat landscape even if they have not been specifically trained how to handle the change. For that, people need to value and care about security on a personal level. The measure of values and caring is the measure of culture.

Can an organization, or even a single security awareness professional, guide the change in the values and culture of an organization? The answer is yes! In this chapter, you will explore the ways that a healthy security culture can grow and how organizations have successfully tackled this challenge. Through research and interviews you will see how the idea of a small group of people, gathering around a central idea, can be the spark that ignites major change in an organization's attitudes toward security.

While it is easier and the chances of success are greater if senior management leads this change, it is not necessary. If you have senior management buy-in or if you are in senior management yourself, this chapter will explain how to leverage this to maximum effect. But if you are the one hoping to change the security culture of senior management, then this chapter can be the blueprint for how to do that, too.

Making Security as Sexy as Brushing Your Teeth

In November 2016, Dashlane asked more than 2,000 people if they would give up sex for a year if it meant that they would never have to worry about being hacked or having their identity stolen. Thirty-nine percent of respondents said yes! While the survey results made for great headlines at the time, there is a deeper story in the responses. People value their security, and there are those who are willing to pay a significant cost for that protection. But one wonders if these same people engage in the secure behaviors and habits that would actually increase their security. It is easy to speculate that they probably do not.

This is not surprising. Regular, daily habits are boring and inconvenient. It would be so much better if the cost could be taken care of all at once. How often have you wondered if getting all your teeth pulled and replaced with dentures would be so much easier than brushing and flossing multiple times a day?

Choosing to value the preservation of the health of what you already have takes strength, knowledge, support, and ongoing investment. Such a value is not held lightly, and it is a hard thing to sell. One-time solutions are much easier to sell than ongoing habits.

It is a common story in a lot of organizations that senior management asks the security department to invest in a project or product that is meant to improve the security and reduce the risks to the organization. This might be a new anti-malware technology, deeper oversight into the network traffic and communications, or a more stringent password policy. Management might approve the project, approve the budget, and accept the inconvenience on behalf of the organization but might also request that they themselves are exempt from any inconvenience (and protection). This is a typical example of a breakdown in security culture. Security is seen as a cost to be minimized, and if possible, a cost borne by others. Security is not seen as a challenge and a struggle to be accepted on a personal level.

A healthy security culture would see senior management demanding that they have more stringent controls than the rest of the organization because they value the protection the controls bring and the unique risks management is under, despite the inconveniences. Sadly, this is not common.

How can you change this? How can you inspire people to share in the ongoing daily struggle of making security a personal value? You can do this by selling the idea of the struggle itself.

Stickers, Lipstick, Joysticks, Sticks

Part of the problem behind why organizations fail to inspire people to accept the challenge of security is the way the challenge is presented. We have all seen the typical way an organization rolls out a new security awareness program. First there is a big marketing campaign where posters, newsletters, branded trinkets, and stickers are passed out to everyone. The hope is to grab attention and to prepare people for a change.

Then the new education program is released and dressed up in as much lipstick as possible to try to disguise the fact that what people are being asked to do is deeply inconvenient and likely confusing. Some organizations try to employ methods, such as those in this book, to reduce resistance to the change process, but they forget that these methods are meant to start a two-way conversation with the individual, not to cram something distasteful into their lives. If organizations attempt this, then the individual becomes distrustful of the message and the messengers.

While some organizations stop after handing out stickers and dressing up the inconvenient, hoping that making the new habits mandatory will carry things through, other organizations take things to the next step and provide training, simulations, and games to try to change each individual's behavior. Because there is a lot of general resistance from people, no program lasts long. Sometimes this results in a long parade of new security awareness and education vendors every couple years or so. Once the parade starts, people stop seeing the actual behaviors being reinforced as something to value, but people notice and compare the quality or features of the different programs. The actual message is lost.

With all this effort and money being invested, management can get quite frustrated if people do not do what they are expected to do. The typical next step in the cycle is to break out the sticks to force people to comply: punishments, shaming, reprimands, fines, and so on. Thankfully, this step in the cycle does not typically last long. Someone usually comes up with the idea to reach out to people on a personal level, make them aware of the issues, and take a friendlier approach. Then they start printing out stickers, and the cycle repeats.

It's no wonder that people think that security awareness and education do not work.

Create a Subculture of Change

There is nothing wrong with stickers or posters or fancy training programs or behavior support training. These are the very things that are advocated in this book! But where organizations can go wrong is trying to use these techniques to force a change that is contrary to the dominant set of values and beliefs of the organization. In short, you can't fight a culture. You will have a never-ending uphill battle if you try to force behaviors on a culture that does not want it.

It is true that over time a strong, consistent insistence on a set of values and behaviors can slowly change a culture, but it takes a very long time and requires leadership from the top over the long term. Some experts estimate that it can take three to ten years for this approach to affect an organization's culture. If those in leadership at the top leave during this period of time, the organization might never fully realize the shift in culture that management desired. But there is a faster way. To quickly and efficiently shift a culture, you need to create a subculture of change for the rest of the main culture to be inspired by and emulate.

Using the methods discussed already in this book, you have the tools you need to raise awareness, educate users, and support behavioral change. But to change a culture, the people have to be open to change. This is different from awareness, education, and behavior because the goal is different. Instead of getting people to know something or getting them to do something, culture change requires that people be open to replacing old ideas with new ones and to be open to the struggles and challenges of trying those ideas. Training and education adds to people's lives. Change replaces things in people's lives and introduces risk and uncertainty.

Change is naturally difficult for people. As you have seen in Maslow's hierarchy of needs, people do things because those things give people something they need on some deep level. You cannot ask them to give up what they are doing just because you asked; instead, you need to show them the benefits of changing and to show them that the risks may not be as high as they think. A simple and effective way to do this is to get a small group of volunteers to try the change first, and then you communicate the successes and pain points those people experience along the way.

A Vocal Team of Interconnected Volunteers

Imagine being responsible to support everyone in your organization to lose five pounds. How much more effective would your efforts be if you asked for a handful of volunteers to be public about their experiences with trying to lose weight this month? You could provide these volunteers with additional and personalized help and attention. As they go through the process, they could blog about what they were doing and feeling that day, whether they were successful in meeting their goals that day or not, and why.

These brave people would become role models for others and an example of how their own experiences could be. The volunteers would also be an example of the things that others might experience, making the others not feel like they were alone or that their experiences were somehow unusual. Someone just like them was experiencing the same thing.

In addition, those volunteers would benefit from the accountability and extra support. As the volunteers experienced problems, they would feel encouraged to express those problems and get the support they needed. The chances for success in this group are maximized, which is useful considering that they are role models for others.

This is the approach that many organizations have used to rapidly and successfully change their cultures. A vocal team of interconnected volunteers from different parts of the organization try something new. Their progress, both positive and negative, is broadcast to the organization as role models to follow. Once people see the effects of adopting a change, they will be far more likely to adopt the new behaviors and values themselves.

Let's delve into the details of how this works.

Find the Big Idea

It is not going to be likely that the average person will accept that a secure behavior has value over and above what they already do enough to instantly change. For instance, you can imagine what people's responses would be if you insisted that everyone use unique, purely random, 20-character strings for all their passwords. That usually takes a lot of convincing at the best of times. The biggest complaint is going to center on the fact that such a complex password is going to be impossible to remember and type. People just want to log in to their computers or their online accounts. They do not want to have to deal with passwords when they have jobs to do or tasks to perform. But if you can tie the idea of a complex password to something they care about more than convenience and ease of use, then you have a chance of making this new idea stick. But what do people care about more than convenience? That is going to be different for different groups of people.

The Five Whys

To find this deeper idea, I like to use the "five whys" technique. This helps me get past the technical details and into more basic motivations. To use this technique, you pose the basic idea, like "use unique, complex passwords," then you ask why someone should accept that idea, and then you ask why about their answer. You repeat this process until you reach a core emotional level.

Here's an example:

"Use unique, complex passwords."
"Why?"
"To make your accounts difficult for other people to access."
"Why do I want to make it difficult for other people to access my accounts?"
"So that malicious people do not gain access to your accounts."
"Why do I not want malicious people to gain access to my accounts?"
"So that they do not get to your money or your personal information."
"Why do I not want malicious people to not get my money or personal information?"
"So that _____."

Those last answers and the last "why" question are the key. Everyone, and every group, is going to answer it differently, and knowing how they might answer those questions is the most important thing in this process. You need to understand what they value and what is most important to them, not what you think is important. Once you get these answers, then you can start crafting a compelling message of change that matches what they care about.

When I was working on a security awareness program for an insurance company, the claims call center had low compliance rates and generally low scores. I set up a meeting with a group of them, and I realized that all of the messages that I crafted for the rest of the company might not be reaching what they cared about. Just before the meeting, I went through the "five whys" process for this particular group of people, and in the end, I had a message to try.

I started the meeting saying this:

> *"You deal with people on the worst day of their month, their year, or sometimes their lives. Don't make their bad day worse by exposing them to viruses or inadvertently leaking their deeply personal information to others."*

It worked. They instantly understood the problem and were on board with learning and applying new secure behaviors. They repeated the phrase "Don't make their bad day worse" as a rallying call between each other, and it was passed on to new members of the team when they joined. With one phrase, that small department changed their security culture, and all I needed to do from then on was to hook into that idea to train and educate them.

The ideas that you need to find should reach so deeply into what people care about that they instantly want to jump on board. However, these ideas might not be about what you expect. The other departments of the insurance company responded to more risk-based messages about limiting impacts of threats, which is not surprising for an insurance company. But the claims department saw the value in empathizing with the customers. The company's policies were not any different, but the perspectives on what the policies were protecting were different.

For maximum effectiveness, the ideas you come up with need to be about something that people deal with on a regular basis and that have an element of urgency. That means people get to be reminded of and get to rehearse the new ideas regularly. The call center agents got to be reminded of the idea "Don't make their bad day worse" every time they answered the phone. If you tie the idea to a value that matters only once a year, for instance, you will lose the feelings of immediacy and urgency that will help propel people to change now instead of changing sometime in the future.

Align to Business Goals

It is vitally important that you align the ideas you come up with to the business goals. If you are in senior management, this will be a lot easier for you than if you are working from the ground up. If you get people to care about an idea that is contrary to what the business wants to do, then you will be fighting the business itself and battling people's deep desire to remain employed. The business will almost always win this fight.

This means you will have to talk to senior management to get a sense of what they want now and what they are going to want in the near future. This might also mean that you will have to go through a "five whys" process just for management, too. Once you do that, though, your chances of getting senior management support increases significantly.

Try to get approval and support from as high up as possible. The chief executive officer (CEO) is best. Aim for the top and slowly work your way down the hierarchy until you find the support you need. In the end, you might find that no one in management wants to support you until they see some sort of success from your proposal. This is not ideal, but I have seen interns successfully change the course of a company with one good idea that everyone in the organization saw value in. Don't be discouraged if you cannot get the support you want. Keep focusing on others and what matters to them.

The idea that will help to change a culture needs to deeply and urgently matter to the people you want to reach, including senior management. But who should you be reaching? Who should the message be reaching first?

Recruit Volunteers

Once you have an idea that resonates so well with people that it will encourage them to replace an idea they already care about, you then need to find people willing to try the new idea in practice. While you might not have the luxury to be picky, there are some volunteers who will be better than others and an unexpected volunteer who you should consider.

Ideally, you are looking for people who are natural leaders. Natural leaders might not hold a position of leadership in your organization but nonetheless have great influence with the people around them. You are also looking for people who are naturally willing to try new things. Often, people who are natural leaders are also those who are eager to try new things, but not always. Your best volunteer has both qualities.

You also want volunteers from as many different areas of the organization and from as many different demographics as possible. You do not want all the volunteers from a single department, for example, or all the same gender or all in the same age range. The best case is that within your volunteers there will be someone who a nonvolunteer can identify with: "She's like me."

The volunteers should also be people who have not already changed their habits and behaviors. They should be going through this change for the first time. This means if you are trying to get the organization to always use the most secure passwords as the systems allows, you should have no one who already does this. It is better if you have people who need to change more than most other people so that others can see the impacts of a big change in behavior.

The unexpected volunteer you should be looking for is a pessimist. The pessimist is someone who is a natural leader, too, but often influencing others to think that new ideas are bad or worth extra scrutiny. You want at least one of these people on your team, if for no other reason than to make sure you are not competing with them. This volunteer will require extra attention and a little extra effort, but this person will also help the diversity of your group so that even other pessimists can see that the idea is not just for the overly optimistic.

Support the Volunteers

Once you have identified these potential volunteers, make it worth their while to be part of this initial team over and above the value of trying the ideas. Again, if you are in management, this is a lot easier, but not necessary. One security awareness professional I know would send a copy of an e-mail to the volunteer's manager when thanking the volunteer for something they did. This meant that being a volunteer had a direct effect on the employee's performance reviews. Storebrand in Norway had senior management support, and volunteers would get a signed letter from the chief security officer (CSO) to thank them for their participation. Rewarding the volunteers is another area where asking the "five whys" can help to uncover what volunteers might value without needing to spend any money if a simple e-mail might suffice instead. Keep in mind that what might work for one group might not work for another. Stay focused on what they value and care about.

To make this volunteer team work well, they will need some form of communication and connection tool. In our current world of having a multitude of connection technologies to choose from, you should have no trouble finding something. The thing to remember is to keep the network limited to just the volunteers. They need this place to share their ideas, try new ideas, and ask for help from each other. It is with this network where one volunteer's efforts can be multiplied by the others.

Even though the volunteers have this isolated place to communicate, make sure they are not working just to benefit themselves and become inwardly focused; instead, make sure everything they do is centered on trying the new ideas and inviting and supporting more and more volunteers to do the same.

Volunteers Draft the Plan

Now that you have a compelling idea that people see the value in and you have connected and supported eager volunteers, the next step is to get the volunteers to convert the idea into an action plan.

You might think that you or management will figure out the best way to put the ideas into action, but this is where a lot of people fail to change the culture. Since you should have a wide range of volunteers from all areas of the organization, use them to come up with the ways that will work for them. They need guidance and direction to make sure that the goals are met and that all the restrictions are respected, but the volunteers need a lot of leeway to design their own program.

If the volunteers come up with an unusual plan, let them try it to see whether it works. As a security professional, you might be too entrenched in your own perspective to see how another perspective might succeed. If you have a diverse group of natural leaders, trust them to lead.

Tell Their Stories

The final and most crucial step in the process is to communicate with the rest of the organization as the volunteers progress. When they have small successes, celebrate those successes and talk about why they were successes. Explore what needed to happen and what needed to change in the volunteers to create those successes. The stories should show how if the volunteers could do it, then everybody else could do it, too.

Equally important is to share the volunteers' failures. Turn the failures into stories and explore why they happened. Follow up by exploring what the volunteer did to bounce back and what changes were made to avoid the failure in the future. If all the stories about the volunteers are positive, the rest of the people might not trust the stories as being "too good to be true." If the volunteers are drafting the action plan themselves, then there will be some experiments that will fall flat, so you should have material to work with.

All these stories and successes are great material to use to check in with management. If you are in senior management, get feedback from the rest of your management team to see what the response has been like and what effects have been seen. You can use this material from management to communicate with the organization. If you are not in senior management, and especially if you have not received strong support from management, let them know about the work the volunteers have done and see whether they might strengthen their support.

One tricky element to telling these stories is deciding how often to share them. It is possible to overwhelm everyone by communicating too frequently, and it is equally possible to get ignored if communicating too infrequently. How you tune your frequency will depend on your organization and the communication channels you use.

Rinse, Repeat

Once the volunteers are experiencing success and communicating to others about it, you should be getting requests from others to join the volunteers. This is ultimately the point of this whole approach, but do not accept them as volunteers right away. Put them on a list, and let them wait a little bit.

The danger of letting everyone volunteer as soon as they want is that the existing volunteers, and their support network, will not be able to handle the flood. Instead, invite subsequent volunteers in stages to let the existing volunteers adjust, figure out the new ideas being brought in by the new volunteers, and work together to refine the plan to reach the rest of the organization.

Then, you simply repeat the entire cycle. Tell the stories of the new volunteers, invite more volunteers, let the team adjust and normalize with the new volunteers, tell their stories, and so on.

At some point, your organization will reach a tipping point where people who are not volunteers will start acting as if they are volunteers, and that is when you know the culture is shifting. The initial volunteers might have needed enticement to try the new ideas, but now the new ideas have been proven, and people are trying them on their own. In the end, you should have a large percentage of the organization that has adopted new values, are engaging in new behaviors, and are encouraging those around them to do the same. It's a total culture shift.

At this point, your security culture program fades and becomes an established support program for the entire organization. Any awareness, education, or training program just needs to tap into these new values to be successful. When new challenges arise, all you need to do is to repeat this process, but it will be even easier because everyone will have seen how well the process works and how it is a powerful force for good while reducing the risks of change for both the individual and the organization.

Will It Work?

Before discussing the research behind this approach and exploring a couple examples where I have personally seen it change large and small groups of people, take a look back at the process and see exactly what your role is in the process. The keen observer will notice that all the work is being done by the volunteers. They draft the plan, they refine the ideas, they reach out to others, and they welcome new volunteers. At a high level, this approach works because the change is organic and happening from within, not dictated by an outside force to look a certain way. This is perhaps the friendliest, most empathetic, most encouraging, and most down-to-earth approach that one could devise. Your role is to support and encourage the volunteers while providing value.

Accelerate

In 1996, John Kotter wrote a groundbreaking book called *Leading Change*. In it, he describes how organizations had successfully led change from within. His model became the core model used by massive organizations to manage change. In 2014, he updated his model in his book *Accelerate*. This book describes how organizations have been able to manage change in the new realities of a rapidly shifting world. *Accelerate* advocates a "two operating system" model for organizations. The first "operating system" is the established, hierarchical system that massive organizations depend on to function and produce consistent results from quarter to quarter and year to year. While this system is great for dependable, long-term results, Kotter says that the system is difficult to use if the organization wants to be able to rapidly adapt to new opportunities. Instead, he advocates a parallel "operating system" that resembles a startup company, using connected volunteers from around the organization who see the value in a big idea that will positively impact the organization, who self-organize, and who bring the idea to life in a form that the hierarchical system can manage efficiently. Sound familiar? I had seen the success of this approach for security culture change before reading Kotter's book, but his research provides some insight into how this approach works for even massive multinational corporations. It is worth a read.

Storebrand Case Study

Storebrand is a 250-year-old company with 2,000 employees across three countries. They had no dedicated security team, and their existing security awareness and education product was a voluntary online course. After auditors assessed that the company needed to address the risks employees present because of errors or poor education, senior management decided to make some big changes. First, they hired a new chief information security officer (CISO), created a small security department, and then brought in an expert in implementing security culture programs, Magnus Solberg.

The goal was to get 66 percent voluntary participation in a security education and culture program without spending a lot of money. While the company needed the security program and the entire function was new, they wanted the program to prove itself in small ways before the company would dedicate a lot of money. To accomplish this feat, Magnus looked for ways to leverage his small team and few funds by recruiting leaders from within Storebrand. To identify these leaders, Magnus surveyed the employees and discovered that the managers were regarded as the natural fit.

Magnus knew that people had access to basic security information, but he wanted to attract people to the new program by offering something people really wanted to know. So, he crafted learning materials to teach people about security threats. Instead of starting with information about what to know and what to do, the material led with an exploration of the things that could go wrong and then covered what they could do about it. The material focused not only on what could go wrong at work but on what things could go wrong at home and in general for different professions. This meant people would learn not only how to secure their employer but also how to be experts in knowing the threats to their families and their own profession.

The managers were given special access to the learning material before it was released to the rest of the company and given advanced material on the program's security topics in case someone in their area had difficult questions. They also had access to the team and each other to provide feedback and bounce ideas off of each other. This special care and attention created highly empowered and motivated leaders who had total freedom to lead their people as they saw fit.

One of the notable leaders was the group CEO who proudly placed a security awareness sticker on his laptop. The CEO also starred in the first videos explaining the new security program and was vocally supportive. It cannot be underestimated how this show of support affected the entire company, but the managers who worked within their area and promoted the program day to day did the real work.

As the program progressed, Magnus and his team sent reports to managers on how many of their employees were participating. These managers started to share their numbers with other managers in a friendly competition between teams. The reports became scorecards and badges of honor for each manager, and the resulting competition spilled down into the teams and resulted in more motivation to participate.

There was so much ground-level support for the program that participation rates were very high. Nine months after the program started and before all the training materials were created, Storebrand saw an 80 percent participation rate, which was far above the goal of 66 percent. After 12 months, the participation rate was 85 percent.

It is worthwhile to note that the security program was first launched in the countries that shared the same business language. Magnus and his team wanted to reduce the complexity and cost of the program by limiting the need for translation and by creating success in one area before tackling the next. When they launched the program in the final country, using the now-tested methods, they saw 80 percent participation rates in the new country within two months.

After 12 months, the program was deemed a huge success. Visits to the internal learning portal are at 200 per month. Employee reporting of potential security events rose from a handful a month to more than 300 per month. There are other effects that are important but difficult to measure. For instance, there is a general attitude of positive feelings about security from the employees, and enviably, the new security department is invited to business meetings for their advice and guidance.

In the most amazing outcome of all, 18 months after the start of the program, a handful of nonsecurity employees started a "security guild" to discuss security matters. After a month, it had 20 members from software developers, sales, and business departments, as well as the data protection officer. The security department is invited to attend.

The security culture at Storebrand fundamentally changed in less than a year. Instead of being an appendix to the employee manual, security is now an integrated part of everyone's lives, promoted and propelled by the employees themselves and not an appointed security department. And it started with a group of empowered volunteers who were given compelling and interesting expertise to share with their peers.

Security Operation Center Case Study

Working in a security operations center (SOC) is demanding work. There are multiple systems to monitor, multiple alerts to respond to, and multiple investigations to launch and competently complete. SOC analysts are tasked with being the front line of defense for the entire organization. They are the "watchers on the wall" who defend everyone, not just those inside the organization but also the innocent people communicating with and conducting business with the organization. Meanwhile, the enemy is ever present and constantly inventing new ways to attack. The cost to the organization is high if the SOC fails.

While there is a lot to do in a security operations center, there are natural lulls where analysts have time to train, learn, and engage in noncritical but valuable additional activities. I worked with one SOC in the United Kingdom to increase analyst participation in a voluntary activity called *threat hunting*.

Threat hunting is when an analyst searches through log data looking for potential threats that the existing detection mechanisms might not have been designed to detect. It is lengthy and often fruitless work, but an analyst's life can get exciting if a potential threat is uncovered. The company wanted to train analysts to perform threat hunting so that they could hunt during lull periods. This was seen as a benefit to all parties: analysts gained on-the-job training and experience in new skill areas, and the organization gained more eyes on unknown threats.

When I started on the project, the most significant feedback we received was that the analysts wanted more training and support. However, despite how much support we designed, we saw a slow decrease in participation for a number of reasons.

First, because of the potential high value in finding a threat, managers were sending only the top analysts for training and support. The external trainers and support frameworks were designed to reach the new analysts. So, there was a mismatch in expectations. Second, because of the high demands on analysts during normal business hours, the appointed hunters were allowed to hunt only on weekends and then were expected to produce output by the following Monday for review. So, hunting became mandatory, and expectations were high. Third, because the trainers and support frameworks were external to the SOC, those who were appointed to hunt had limited access to personal support, and even less support than otherwise expected because they were hunting when the experts were not in the office.

At one point, when I asked analysts about what they thought about hunting and the support they were receiving, they said something like, "What? You want us to do more work?" Then, at a meeting with a manager, I was told, "Hunting used to be seen as something fun. All the fun has been taken out of it."

What was intended to be a support for people to happily engage in a career-enhancing, voluntary activity was being regarded as a rigid policy and procedure manual being imposed by an absent dictator. The reason this was not caught earlier was that every time I asked, everyone had such a positive view of hunting as a concept. What I missed was that the frameworks put in place to assist the hunters were being regarded as a hindrance, and people were afraid to say so. I recommended that everyone take a step back and let everything cool off while we figured out another approach.

At about the same time, the internal champion for threat hunting left the SOC, and another analyst stepped into the voluntary role as well as being promoted. The new champion was so overwhelmed with getting up to speed on all the new duties of his job that he was too busy to engage in the hunting process as intended. So, he made changes in order to free up time to do his regular duties.

First, instead of choosing hunters and giving them defined hunts to perform, he chose four different hunting types, with examples, and ranked them in terms of difficulty. Then he posted them for any analyst to attempt at any time. Second, because it was unassigned and voluntary, the requirement for review was dropped, which eliminated any expectations about quality. Third, instead of the detailed guidance, he created five high-level questions the analyst needed to be able to answer by the time the hunt was deemed complete. Fourth, he made himself available to personally help anyone who asked, and because of the nature of the SOC, this help was public and delivered in a way that everyone could hear while they did their normal duties.

The results from these changes were amazing. Using the provided examples, one analyst quickly discovered something interesting, which kicked off a formal investigation. When this success was communicated to the SOC the next day, many more analysts started working their way through the four example hunts until almost all analysts had made some attempt on their own that week. This was an unprecedented level of participation, so we let this new system carry on to see where it would take us.

After two months, the investigative team of the organization outside of the SOC was making comments in meetings about the high-quality findings and investigations performed by the SOC as a result of hunting. An on-the-job training program was put together, and there were more analysts demanding to participate than the program could handle. In those two months, the majority of new analysts on the team had engaged in threat hunting at some point in the eight-week period where, previously, few had attempted any hunting at all. SOC managers reported seeing an increase in the quality of the normal investigative activities of analysts, too.

Two months after that, the SOC had been transformed. Analysts were starting to self-identify as threat hunters who also did security analysis. Every single analyst in the SOC was engaging in hunting activities on a regular basis. Analysts who were seen as having stalled in their careers were now considered the superstars in the SOC with bright futures. Analysts themselves, including new, untrained analysts, were voluntarily taking it upon themselves to maintain the internal documentation site that supported the hunting activities, just to be involved somehow. All of the external experts who had been supporting threat hunting in the SOC deemed themselves superfluous. The culture had changed, and it was now self-supporting.

Technically, nothing was different in the new approach. Hunts were still prechosen for the analysts, and outputs were still being reviewed for quality. In fact, less time was assigned to the hunters to hunt. But perceptions were vastly different. The analysts felt that they had choice and autonomy, and the people reviewing the output were not threat-hunting experts checking quality, but rather they were the next level of investigators who demanded a certain level of quality in order to take on the investigation. Because the leader provided examples, there was a perception that the examples themselves had a higher value than any starting activity that an analyst could come up with on their own.

In summary, the analysts were perceived to have more control, help was personal and immediate, no one was grading them on their performance or even expecting them to participate, and the value of the activity was translated into real, personal value. The more the value was realized and shown to have positive impact, the more people wanted to get involved. The result was a complete culture change across 100 percent of the department, and the benefit to the organization of this culture change can be quantifiably measured in terms of discovered threats and reduced risk.

CHAPTER 8

Take Your Program to the Next Level

Security awareness programs can be wonderfully challenging, but the benefits of a truly effective awareness program are worth every bit of effort. Security awareness programs do not need to be 100 percent effective, and they never will be, because each incident involves a fallible human making a choice in the moment. Our jobs as trainers are to equip each person for that moment of decision and to support them afterward, regardless of the outcome. Doing this, we can reach new levels of effectiveness, retention, compliance, and maturity for our security awareness programs.

Programs that emphasize only the knowledge-based information or the content of the security policies will go stale quickly, and it is unlikely that such programs will result in changed behaviors. Instead of putting all your efforts into making incremental changes to the material itself, it is more effective if your security awareness program includes ways of supporting your users as they develop secure habits and tests those habits consistently over time. Active feedback and persistent training are efficient ways to do that, and these methods do not have to be expensive or complex.

Active feedback uses a user's natural inclination to want to develop new habits by using the elements of sport and games to support experimentation and self-discovery. Letting users feel like they have developed their own methods of achieving their security goals results in much higher levels of compliance because users feel like they are complying with their own rules and not someone else's. Supporting user-generated habits requires that the awareness trainer think beyond the classroom, or computer-based training, to think about building personal relationships and being more personally involved in users' daily lives. While this might be difficult for an awareness team to accomplish in a large organization, recruiting the assistance of help-desk and incident response personnel can extend the reach of an active feedback initiative. As an added benefit, active feedback produces informative metrics that can provide deeper insights into the secure habits, and even the security culture, of an organization.

© Jordan Schroeder 2017
J. Schroeder, *Advanced Persistent Training*, DOI 10.1007/978-1-4842-2835-7_8

Persistent training extends the impact of a security awareness program year-round. Breaking up the training materials into graduated modules that users can explore at their own pace keeps the material engaging. Graduated modules are also likely to encourage users to reach beyond the basic requirements of organizational policy and procedure and into more advanced material. Testing users on their security habits while the user is performing their normal daily tasks has a much higher chance of reinforcing the learning objectives. Dynamically spacing out the testing as users succeed and fail will help to ensure that users are getting the training they need, at a pace that is appropriate for them.

In combination, active feedback and persistent training can improve knowledge retention, increase compliance, increase engagement, decrease resistance, and take your security awareness program to the next levels of effectiveness.

APPENDIX A

■ ■ ■

Lessons from the Masters

The following insights are from companies that perform security awareness training in various forms. These companies are on the leading edge of security awareness training, and they are defining the state of the art in effective approaches, techniques, and tools. These companies generously consented to interviews where they were asked questions about how they approach security awareness training and what tips they could pass on to you.

Wombat Security Technologies

www.WombatSecurity.com

Jordan Schroeder: Who is Wombat Security Technologies?

Joe Ferrara, CEO: Wombat Security Technologies provides information security awareness and training software to help organizations teach their employees secure behavior. Our SaaS-based cyber-security education solution includes a platform of integrated broad assessments, as well as a library of simulated attacks and interactive microlearning training modules. Wombat Security Technologies' solutions help organizations reduce successful phishing attacks and malware infections by up to 90 percent. For two years in a row, we have been recognized as a leader in the Gartner Magic Quadrant for Security Awareness Computer-Based Training Vendors, and we are helping Fortune 1000 and Global 2000 customers in industry segments such as finance and banking, energy, technology, higher education, retail, and consumer packaged goods to strengthen their cyber-security defenses.

© Jordan Schroeder 2017

J. Schroeder, *Advanced Persistent Training*, DOI 10.1007/978-1-4842-2835-7

JS: What would you say is your unique approach or philosophy in security awareness training?

JF: At Wombat, we have developed a unique continuous training methodology based on established learning science principles. Our platform blends interactivity, storytelling, immediate feedback, and other proven educational techniques that are critical to knowledge retention and long-term behavior change.

We take a 360-degree view of awareness and training, and our approach integrates assessments (via topic-focused questionnaires and simulated social engineering attacks), education (via interactive and game-based modules), reinforcement techniques (via licensed posters, newsletters, and giveaways), and measurement (via data collection from assessments, education, and user input).

We encourage all our customers to think beyond programs that only use simulated phishing attacks and/or infrequent and nonengaging training sessions via methods such as presentations and videos. This is because the *and* in "security awareness and training" can be the differentiator between a successful program and lackluster results. Making users aware that a problem such as phishing exists is not the same as teaching them how to apply best practices in their day-to-day routines and how to make the right decisions in risky situations.

JS: How do you implement "gamification" in your training program?

JF: Several of the training modules we offer would be considered "game-based training" in the traditional sense, in that they utilize lives, scores, and time. But the rest of our modules also feature what we feel is the most important aspect of gamification in training: interactivity.

All of our training modules actively engage users and allow them to practice what they've learned. Key interactivity features include drag-and-drop sorting, password practice, scenario-based decision-making, and "day-in-the-life" progressions. With noninteractive presentations, users can easily tune out or shift focus to other activities while videos run. Interactivity enables engagement, and an engaged participant is far more likely to remember what they're taught. And as we all know, knowledge retention is the key to any successful education program.

JS: What challenges have you faced when integrating into an organization's culture?

JF: One (somewhat surprising) cultural challenge we faced in our organization's early days was related to simulated phishing attacks. We learned that many organizations were not comfortable sending mock attacks to their employees. This also meant, however, that they were missing the key benefit that simulated attacks provide: the capability to measure the vulnerability of the users within their organizations.

Because we understand the importance of assessing knowledge levels and establishing a baseline measurement of susceptibility, we accepted the challenge of developing a tool that would allow organizations to evaluate their employees' recognition of phishing threats. But we took it a step further by enabling assessments of other security-related issues in all threat areas, including safe use of mobile devices, physical security safeguards, and proper use of passwords.

Out of this challenge came our CyberStrength Knowledge Assessment product, which offers administrators a library of questions about a number of cyber-security topics, including compliance matters. We also allow administrators to craft their own questions so they can get a sense of how well their employees understand organizational policies and known issues. This portfolio is tightly integrated with our training modules, which means we can effectively educate users about the concepts they have the most trouble grasping.

By eliminating this cultural barrier, we made it possible for all our customers to effectively assess their employee base prior to, and during, an awareness and training program, a step that is essential to measuring progress and gauging results.

JS: What noteworthy reasons have you heard about why users resist awareness training?

JF: If we're honest, we don't believe there are any "noteworthy" reasons for resisting training. Education is critical to the advancement of people and ideas in virtually every space; why not cyber-security? That said, we certainly do come across people who question whether awareness training is "worth it," even though these same people have benefited extensively from training in order to be more effective at their jobs. Generally, these are also the same people who tend to regard "perfection" as the only adequate result for security awareness and training. Technical safeguards fail all the time; we would never suggest they be eliminated from an organization's security posture. Why take away an opportunity to make your users more savvy about cyber-hygiene and make them part of your defense against attack?

That said, we know that some organizations are resistant to training. Often, we hear concerns about taking time and attention away from employees' "day jobs." We certainly recognize that organizations are spread thin from a resources perspective. This is a prime reason we advocate for "bitesize" training assignments served at regular intervals (10 minutes here, 15 minutes there) that employees can work into their schedules as they have time. This is far more efficient than half-day or daylong training sessions that can cause disruptions department- or organization-wide for days at a time. In addition, educated employees are less likely to suffer from malware infections and other equipment downtime, which, in turn, means that IT resources are less consumed with fire drills and device cleanup.

JS: Do you think that a reward system works in security awareness training?

JF: We definitely believe in positive reinforcement techniques; in fact, they are a foundational element of our "assess, educate, reinforce, measure" continuous training methodology. Employees are far more receptive to training when they feel they are being empowered rather than shamed. When rewards are incorporated into a program, it seems to invigorate employees and make them more attentive and engaged.

We encourage, and help, our customers to recognize departments and individuals who are making positive strides and serving as good examples to others. Our PhishAlarm e-mail reporting button makes employees an active part of an organization's cyber-security defense system, and anyone who reports a suspected phishing message is immediately recognized with a pop-up display or e-mail thanking them for their efforts and encouraging them to continue to monitor their inboxes for suspicious messages. In addition, our security awareness materials, another part of our reinforcement product offering, include options for small gifts and giveaways that our customers can use to reward good behaviors.

PhishLine

www.PhishLine.com

Jordan Schroeder: Who is PhishLine?

Mark Chapman, CEO: PhishLine performs millions of security awareness training exercises worldwide each year, including traditional computer-based training, mock social engineering tests, and risk-based surveys using our proven "plan, train, test, measure, and take action" methodology. Since 2011, millions of people have engaged with PhishLine's unique risk-based platform.

JS: What would you say is your unique approach or philosophy in security awareness training?

MC: As part of a risk-based continuous improvement process, the results of an effective information security awareness program should provide actionable observations to improve the people, processes, and technology layers of security controls.

We do not believe in a one-size-fits-all approach to training. We also do not believe that training is the only or best solution in all cases. While training can be effective, the level of effectiveness is dynamic. Training methods must be objectively measured and adjusted over time to ensure success. An effective training program must be synchronized with changes to the technical and process control environment to enable the most powerful and efficient combination to mitigate certain threats.

A big component that makes our approach unique is the emphasis on hypothesis-based testing. Rather than depending solely on external studies and benchmarks, our customers leverage specific tests to improve the security posture of their organization.

A simple example is the hypothesis that "users are more likely to click e-mails in their native language than in English." Before designing a test to validate the hypothesis, it is imperative to identify what actions will be taken if the test results support the hypothesis, negate the hypothesis, or are inconclusive.

If you cannot identify meaningful actions, there is little justification for performing the test. Risk-based methods should be used to identify more actionable tests.

We strongly feel that hypothesis-based testing is a critical component to any security awareness program. It provides context, ensures relevance, and enables appropriate remediation actions based on the resulting metrics.

JS: If you use "gamification" in your training program, how have you implemented it?

MC: Gamification can be applied to several levels of an information security awareness training program.

A basic approach is to integrate gaming elements directly into security awareness training materials with the hope of adding excitement to traditional computer-based training. Sometimes these things are engaging and fun. Other times, they are viewed as trivial or childish and can quickly reduce the credibility of your overall program. The corporate culture, geographic location, and age groups involved make a huge difference in how this style of content is perceived. We provide many styles of training directly through our Content Center Marketplace and through our content partners. Gamification may or may not be the best way to increase engagement rates and effectiveness.

Another way that we use gamification is through a customer-defined risk-based scoring system. Customers can set point values for positive and negative actions. They can then compare risk-based scores to internal and external benchmarks and measure improvements over time.

Generally, customers assign negative points to unsafe actions such as the following:

- Clicked a link or filled in a web form

- Replied to an e-mail or text message or disclosed too much information in automated out-of-office replies

- Called an unknown phone number in an e-mail or plugged an unapproved portable media device into a business computer

In a similar manner, customers assign positive points to positive actions such as the following:

- Completed training

- Reported a suspicious e-mail using the correct channels

- Hung up on a phone call before disclosing sensitive information

Customers use these metrics to look at the results of individual campaigns and to analyze trends. The scores can be arbitrarily grouped to enable custom dashboards to drive a competitive spirit that fits the specific culture and goals of the organization.

JS: What challenges have you faced when integrating into an organization's culture?

MC: At the basic level, everyone initially struggles with selecting appropriate themes for the mock social engineering exercises. The frequency of tests, the sophistication of tests, the pre-announcement of tests, the number of people to test, what level of results to share, and other common issues need to be addressed.

Beyond the basics, the biggest cultural challenges we face are misguided metrics and too much focus on a small number of solution choke points.

Many information security awareness programs become obsessed with one and only one metric: the click-through rate. This easy-to-understand metric represents the percent of people who clicked a link in a particular campaign e-mail. To be fair, much of the marketing in this industry historically focused on reducing click-through rates.

This myopic view ignores the fact that not all clicks are created equal from a risk perspective. If a user clicks a link, then submits a login and password, and then uploads a budget spreadsheet, is that the same risk than if they just clicked a link and closed a landing page? Are there other risky actions a user can take other than clicking? Many attackers are using attachments and other techniques to perform social engineering. You can learn a lot by performing a mock phishing campaign that has no links whatsoever. The call to action can be to solicit an e-mail reply or to direct the user to a different vector, such as calling a phone number.

One of our customers made the analogy that measuring the success of a security awareness program by looking only at raw click-through rates is just like measuring the success of a patch management program by looking at the number of new vulnerabilities found each month.

Metrics must be contextual, relevant, and actionable. For a vulnerability management solution, the raw number of patches is much less interesting than the average time to patch. For a phishing program, putting raw click-through rates in the context of hypothesis-based testing and risk-based observations will allow much better, more actionable metrics. "We learned this, we validated that, we discovered this, and we adjusted that."

The second biggest challenge is the tendency to put too much focus on a small number of solution choke points. Early on, programs tend to exclusively focus on the "teachable moment."

While there is good supporting evidence that the teachable moment can be the most effective single approach, there are many easily identifiable scenarios where alternative approaches may be more effective.

- The "five-second rule" is where users quickly close their browsers in the hopes that they were quick enough that the click did not count and they do not need to take the in-the-moment training. How can you identify those users and apply a different approach?

- Although it may be the teachable moment, some users are not exactly in a "teachable mood" right after you tell them that they have just been duped. How can you change your approach to provide an opportunity for positive behavior modification for those users?

- Finally, you need to be careful you are not training your employees to be excellent "mock phishing detectors." By performing tests that do not have a teachable moment, you may find additional insights into user behavior in a broader variety of real-world scenarios.

There is more to life than click-through rate. The same thing goes for incident response reporting rates or other single-focused raw metrics. These are all important components to an effective program. The raw metrics just have limited value on a stand-alone basis.

Ultimately, your information security awareness program should be measured based on the answer to the question, "How many risk-based observations have led to measurable remediation of controls at the people, process, and technology layers?"

JS: What noteworthy reasons have you heard about why users resist awareness training?

MC: Training is too boring, technical, childish, cartoonish, ominous, or any number of other subjective measures.

Training is incomplete, inconsistent, or contradictory. Training users to mouse over a link is of limited use to mobile device users who need to use the click-hold method. Remember when it was standard advice to instruct users to always unsubscribe from spam e-mails? More recent examples of contradictory training happens when the URL-rewrite capabilities of various spam filtering solutions no longer allow users to see the actual URL in an e-mail before clicking.

Training does not work on a device or in a work environment. A lack of speakers or the ability to use them in an office without disturbing co-workers is a valid consideration. Bandwidth requirements for multimedia training or lack of plug-in support for tablets and mobile devices can be a real problem, with similar issues for obsolete desktop hardware. The solution is to plan ahead, test, and provide multiple versions of training to accommodate various technical limitations.

Poorly translated multimedia materials can be frustrating, especially for languages with strongly divergent regional dialects. Be sure to have users in each region review the materials before deploying. The subtle nature of many security awareness training concepts can easily get lost in translation. From a scheduling perspective, be aware of local holidays before sending out campaigns and realize that current events at the local level can introduce unexpected, even offensive, interpretations of proven training content. Establish a clear feedback loop to quickly adjust content.

Finally, some people fundamentally believe training does not work. They eagerly cite examples like, "If training worked, then there would be no car accidents because we all passed driver's education." Of course, training is not a 100 percent solution, but can you imagine if all those other drivers had never taken driver's education? In the information security awareness context, you can and must objectively measure the effectiveness of specific training content on specific subsets of your target audience. Expect the results to change over time.

There are solutions to all of these problems, which should be addressed during the formal planning process with comprehensive checklists and feedback channels to guide the continuous improvement process.

JS: Do you think that a reward system works in security awareness training?

MC: At the individual employee level, what works or does not greatly depends on the culture of the organization and the age, background, and job role of the various groups of employees.

The most interesting pattern for success we see is when organizations align the security awareness training reward system with the most effective incentive systems engrained in the business.

Is your organization metrics-driven? We have seen great success where managers at every level of an organization include a security awareness scorecard every month as part of their overall metrics scorecards. Of course, the managers need to see how this helps them be more effective rather than it being punitive. Work with them to find out what they are most afraid of happening in the business. If that is susceptible to happening because of a social or cyber-attack, they are more likely to embrace your program as a solution to their problem rather than a distraction.

Is your organization audit-driven? We have seen great success where results of the awareness program were put in terms of formal observations or risk-based audit findings with observation descriptions, potential business impact statements, recommendations, and the whole audit-committee-style management response mechanisms.

Is your organization profit-driven? Quality-driven? Figure out how things actually get done and model the reward system for information security after the most effective reward system at the company.

Is there a similar program that has been effective? We have seen companies emulate effective safety programs as the model for a security awareness program. This does not mean they are merged. It simply means that if your organization values safety, talk to the safety director to see how success is measured, communicated, and rewarded.

Ultimately, the most consistent path to success is to tightly integrate the reward at all levels with the rest of the business reward structure to take advantage of the tone at the top and to align the existing management structure to support the program because it provides real business value.

JS: What is an example of a situation where your training ended up being a much bigger success than you expected?

MC: The security awareness team at a large organization decided to leverage the "tone at the top" to encourage people to be more aware. They produced a professional video of the CEO talking through what phishing is, why it is a threat to the organization, and what he expected people to do about it. He specifically stated that mock phishing tests would be performed by PhishLine, and while he could not expect perfection, he made it clear that users would not want to get on the repeat offender list.

The "before" and "after" picture was a dramatic improvement on a sustainable basis because of a clear, consistent, strong tone at the top. Security is critically important to this organization and to the CEO. This one simple video had a bigger measurable impact than all the prior announcements, threats, rewards, and prizes.

Rapid7

RAPID7

www.Rapid7.com

Jordan Schroeder: Who is Rapid7?

Todd Lefkowitz, vice president of professional services: Rapid7 is engineering better security with simple, innovative solutions for IT security's most critical challenges. The company's security data and analytics solutions collect, contextualize, correlate, and analyze the security data its customers need to dramatically reduce threat exposure and detect compromise in real time. Rapid7's security awareness curricula combines learning theory and subject-matter expertise to deliver an online course that is informative and compelling. These highly interactive scenario-based modules equip employees to recognize the value of different types of information; to understand the scope, nature, and origin of the diverse risks to such information; and to behave proactively to protect this information in their everyday work.

JS: What would you say is your unique approach or philosophy in security awareness training?

TL: Our approach is to promote modularization, topic relevancy, and interactivity. Additionally, we provide supplemental and customizable content such as articles, tip sheets, infographics, and templates that can be leveraged by our customers to drive adoption and/or create specialized corporate-wide campaigns. We also offer a more flexible consumption model that allows customers to run on their own or through a hosted/cloud solution.

JS: How do you implement "gamification" in your training program?

TL: First, we use modularized, interactive "learning moments" that are little exercises that reinforce the behaviors learned in earlier training modules. Instead of being presented as assessments, they are mini-games that capture the user's attention to focus on specific topics. We find this method much more approachable and more engaging than videos and a better way to gauge a user's understanding than a multiple-choice test, which tends to be too easy and not a great test of retention.

Of course, in addition to the security awareness program modules and learning moments, we recommend that organizations use Metasploit Pro to launch simulated phishing attacks on the users of the organization as a true test of its susceptibility to attacks.

We have found that it takes a minimum of three training sessions for the material to sink in. If you plan for the need for repetition, you can optimize how, and what, you repeat. For example, some organizations assess their users first with a simulated phishing attack, follow up with training, and then assess again. By doing it this way, they gain an "extra" repetition of the training by starting with the assessment before the user is trained.

JS: What challenges have you faced when integrating into an organization's culture?

TL: Integrating awareness training into the organization's culture is all about getting the users engaged and integrating training and testing as a normal business process. When people are thinking about awareness training as a typical business activity, then training interleaves with the culture pretty naturally.

Cultural issues aren't confined to organizational culture. When we prepared translations for training materials for international customers in the past, we ran into situations where the accents of the voice actors were an issue in one country and where the color schemes had an unintended cultural significance in another. If you are preparing training materials for a company with offices in other countries, take these potential issues into account and run your materials past knowledgeable people in those areas as early in the development process as possible.

JS: What noteworthy reasons have you heard about why users resist awareness training?

TL: We really don't see users actively resisting awareness training. If you look at industry statistics, such as the annual Verizon Data Breach report, you will see that the leading attack vectors are phishing, user credentials, and social engineering. Security awareness training is designed specifically to close those gaps and to safeguard against human compromise. Our customers realize that educating the human custodians of their data and assets is crucial to the security of their organizations. For the most part, the companies we speak with realize there are some amazing security solutions on the market; however, if you don't have competent people managing those solutions and the right supporting processes in place, it doesn't really matter how good your technology is. In the end, it's not really a question of whether companies will adopt security awareness but whether they build or buy. Threat landscape conditions demand it.

JS: Do you think that a reward system works in security awareness training?

TL: Scores can be an effective reward system. When people are confronted with competition or if they are rated against their peers, they instinctively behave differently. No one wants to see themselves slipping down a Top Users list, and people want to try to get on one. If you do post Top Users lists, don't post the Bottom Users lists or post a list of where every user ranks in the organization. Be careful not to publicly shame users because it will backfire.

Some organizations can get very creative with their rewards and punishments with success. One organization I know posted bounties for noncompliant behaviors, such as not securing laptops. Employees were rewarded $25 for taking and turning in laptops that were not physically locked. The mild shame a user felt of having to go to the security department to retrieve their laptop was more than enough to make sure it didn't happen again, and the bounty made all employees extra aware of everyone else's secure behaviors.

Recognition and rewards programs can also work, and many mature organizations have programs like this already in place. What you have to watch out for is that the existing programs do not get overloaded with the flood of work that is required to make recognition and rewards worthwhile to include in awareness training. If you do have a recognition and rewards program like this in place, don't pass off all the metrics and reporting to that team. Only the awareness administrator can fully understand the meaning of certain metrics.

Curricula

www.GetCurricula.com

Jordan Schroeder: Who is Curricula?

Nick Santora, CEO: Curricula is a new organization that takes traditional concepts from brand awareness and applies it to security awareness. Our team has a diverse background in advertising, marketing, cyber-security, compliance, audit, and education. We use a simple approach to convert learners through automated campaigns to deliver a unique experience that engages learners.

JS: What would you say is your unique approach or philosophy in security awareness training?

NS: Curricula uses story-based learning to engage learners through our campaigns. Our goal in aware campaigns is designed to connect with our learners on a personal level first. As you travel through an aware experience, you are presented with interactive experiences that engage you on the story being told and not just about security content. Each story uses characters, animations, and a detailed storyline that describes the scenario being discussed. We learn at a young age through storytelling, so we take the same approach and deliver an educational experience like no other.

The production quality behind our campaigns is very high. Our team puts so much effort not only into the content but into building the storyline, the characters, the colors, music, and everything else that plays a role in the user experience. It is that quality and expertise of delivery that is unique to Curricula.

JS: What challenges have you faced when integrating into an organization's culture?

NS: Most organizations have a linear approach when it comes to training or security awareness. Training usually consists of dumping videos or slides onto their users at the end of the year, along with HR paperwork and a few other "check the box" activities. Security awareness training shouldn't be one of them. Our approach is to educate our clients first on the purpose of security awareness, its goals, and the ROI that quality education places on the organization.

This is typically a difficult discussion because most organizations do not provide enough funding, resources, or support for cyber-security education programs. Most budget money is spent on the latest and greatest firewalls, security appliances, and other technology, hoping that users do not need to be relied on. This is a fundamentally flawed approach because setting a strong foundation of cyber-security education can be the difference between a successful attack and a prevented incident. Empowering your users with education will never cease to have an impact, and it continues to be the best ROI for preventing cyber-attacks.

JS: What noteworthy reasons have you heard about why users resist awareness training?

NS: It's a behavior that has been around for so long. As soon as the word *training* is mentioned, an unconscious behavior is made to immediately ignore the material that is about to be presented. This is from past experiences and an understanding that this will be similar to a past experience. Training is treated as punishment, and it is sad to see that approach by many companies we have spoken with. By changing the experience, you can change interest, and by changing interest, you can change behavior.

JS: Do you think that a reward system works in security awareness training?

NS: I spoke to one organization that did phishing against their own company. They said that if a user is a contractor and clicks a link in their mock attack, the contractor is immediately fired. Subsequently, if a staff member clicks a link, they are suspended for a day. I have even talked to companies that reward a learner by offering $200 or more if they do not get phished by the mock attempt. What happened? In both scenarios, the results were more than 50 percent of the staff were *still* caught in phishing attacks. So, there is no silver bullet in implementing rewards or penalties that replaces education. The goal should be to focus on connecting with your users and delivering quality content that will help improve their behaviors.

How to Implement Third-Party Training

I asked each of these security awareness companies what advice they would give a security awareness trainer who was interested in implementing a third-party training provider into their organization. The following is what they had to say.

Wombat Security Technologies' Joe Ferrara

"We feel there are enormous benefits to utilizing third-party training over internal training. Many organizations simply don't have the resources or expertise in house to develop tools that are research-driven, fully integrated, and updated frequently to reflect the ever-evolving threat landscape. As well, relying on an internal vision can be limiting; it's often difficult to step out of the immediacy of day-to-day issues and get a sense of the bigger picture that is employee-based cyber-security risk. Coming at the problem with an internal, tunnel-like focus can cause organizations to miss out on key opportunities to change behaviors and reduce risk.

"We really encourage our customers to think beyond single-tool programs. If they're only doing simulated phishing attacks, they're missing out on the opportunity to truly educate their employees. Similarly, if they're only using training messages, they're missing out on the chance to assess and evaluate how employees respond in situations that mirror real-world attacks. A combination of assessments, education, reinforcement techniques, and measurement give organizations the variety they need to keep a program fresh and effective over the long term.

"There has been an overreliance on videos and instructional presentations in the training space, particularly with compliance-related topics. We get it; these tools feel like "the path of least resistance," and they seem to offer a quick, easy way to check the box on compliance training. But videos and presentations, though good informational tools, are not effective educational tools. Studies have shown that users tune out during noninteractive training situations. If users are not paying attention, they have no hope of learning anything, and organizations have no hope of seeing measurable results from their training. Without interactivity, users are far less likely to be engaged and far less likely to retain knowledge. So, it's easy to see why video- and presentation-based programs have a bad rap for being ineffective. Change that approach by utilizing third-party training, like Wombat's, that puts users in the driver seat, allowing them to set the pace, make decisions, and engage with the content. This is key to driving results."

PhishLine's Mark Chapman

"Leveraging third-party security awareness programs is a great way to shorten the learning curve, quickly establish credibility, and hasten the return on investment. Dedicated vendors can provide a broad set of experience, innovative tools, and robust data that can help programs be more successful today and into the future. To maximize success, you must select the right vendor in the context of a dynamic, objectives-based program.

"The following are important factors to consider when selecting a vendor.

"Are you looking for an education-only platform, or would you like the ability to combine both threat simulation and training? If all you need is an education platform, there are many more vendors that can service those limited needs. Integrated platforms simplify the follow-up process, validate the effectiveness of campaign content, streamline reporting, and future-proof the investment.

"Is your vision to test e-mail phishing only, or would you like to be able to conduct voice, SMS, and mobile media attack simulations? While all vendors have some of these components, each will have their particular strength. The ultimate goal is to choose a fully integrated platform that includes completely automated social engineering vectors with robust educational content.

"What particular security, privacy, and/or regulatory considerations need to be met by the prospective partner? There is a lot of variation when it comes to security, with options ranging from software that is hosted on shared public cloud infrastructure to highly secure dedicated hosting facilities. Some vendors provide options for on-premise deployment.

"Do you want the vendor to provide hosting of your own training content? Vendors who can host SCORM-compliant content can provide flexibility that can allow you to focus on the content and let the vendor handle the hosting. There are also options where you can host vendor training content on your existing learning management system.

"Will you require significant customization of the training content? Customization capabilities and costs widely vary between vendors. Many allow you to incorporate your own branding, logos, and styles. The ability to customize the actual curriculum with your specific message is another important consideration.

"Does the vendor provide third-party content from other security awareness providers to broaden the training catalog? Training content needs to be fresh and objective. A one-stop shop can provide depth without introducing new vendor relationships.

"Is malware analysis and centralized phishing reporting a requirement? Do you require a plug-in for your e-mail client? If so, what e-mail clients require support? Many vendors provide options. The lines are starting to blur between awareness vendors and incident response solutions. Be sure to consider if a best-of-breed or an all-in-one approach is the most appropriate for your environment.

"Do you have specific reporting requirements? It seems every vendor allows reporting data to be exported to Excel. Are you required to perform extensive gymnastics in Excel to get the data you need? Look for a vendor that allows for custom reporting and analysis in a format that is ready for you to use.

"Are there other systems or data sources that you would like to integrate with the testing and training platform? Risk-based solutions tend to work better with more data. Vendors provide several approaches, which may help take your program to the next level by extending the teachable moments to the teachable moments that matter. API options can help you leverage the data and capabilities otherwise trapped in a vendor solution.

"While this list is not exhaustive, it will help you narrow down your search to a few providers and will help you focus on the key capabilities you require to make *your* program successful.

"The best advice is to recognize that a successful program is dynamic and must have clear goals and objectives. Leverage the vendors that most deeply align with your current and future objectives."

Rapid7's Todd Lefkowitz

"Generally speaking, it's cheaper to buy security awareness training than to build. Enlisting a third party, whose job it is to focus intently on security awareness, will not only be diligent in innovation to stay ahead of competitors but also be active in ensuring content is kept fresh and relevant.

"Third parties also have greater access and economies of scale when it comes to rollout and localization on a global scale. Translation can be exceptionally expensive, and third-party vendors can significantly lessen the financial burden to their customers with the inclusion of language packages within their solutions. If a vendor you like doesn't have a language you require, they may be willing to make the investment without an up-charge to translate, knowing that it will be a reusable commodity after your purchase.

"A lot of companies are migrating to the cloud, and security awareness vendors are certainly among them. Some vendors allow their learning modules to be run through a learning management system. Picking a vendor that allows for this will streamline onboarding and use of the solution; it negates having to learn an entirely new system. Furthermore, if you're already accustomed to a learning management system, you will be familiar with the reporting formats, reducing costs, since they reduce hosting fees.

"A solid phishing simulation tool is a must as well. It's a great way to really assess the efficacy of training and how well your employees adopt the content through their training experience. If the third party does not have a phishing simulation tool, then a product like Rapid7's Metasploit Pro can be leveraged to generate phishing campaigns pre- and post-training."

Curricula's Nick Santora

"There are a lot of great tools and services out there. With cloud services becoming a popular option, it is easy to find expert third-party organizations that can perform a function for your business at fractions of the time, cost, and effort. Take accounting software, for example. There are plenty of companies out there that can handle your books, transactions, integrations, and management, all with a few simple clicks.

"Likewise, third-party security awareness teams are an excellent option for businesses to leverage the resources and development of a focused service. At Curricula, all we do is cyber-security awareness training. We don't do consulting work, we don't sell widgets, we simply focus on teaching people cyber security. In today's world, taking advantage of your core competencies can mean the difference between staying in business and floundering. Getting flooded with wasted resources, stressed-out staff, and an unclear plan on how to deliver security awareness training can be easily avoided by engaging a third-party security awareness team who is ready to execute a proven plan."

References

Aaron Dignan. Game Frame. Free Press, New York, NY, 2011.

Abraham Maslow. Toward a Psychology of Being. Wiley and Sons, New York, NY, 3rd edition, 1998.

Charles Coonradt. The Game of Work. Gibbs Smith, United States, 2012.

Dave Aitel. Why you shouldn't train employees for security awareness. CSO Online, July 2012. http://www.csoonline.com/article/2131941/security-awareness/why-you-shouldn-t-train-employees-for-security-awareness.html.

Jaikumar Vijayan. Phishing emerges as major corporate security threat. Network World, April 2011. http://www.networkworld.com/article/2202359/security/phishing-emerges-as-major-corporate-security-threat.html.

John Leyden. Half of phish marks respond to scams within one 'golden hour'. The Register, December 2010. http://www.theregister.co.uk/2010/12/03/phishing_response_survey/.

Karen Pryor. Don't Shoot the Dog! Bantam, San Francisco, USA, 1999.

Karen Pryor. Hidden aversives: Are you punishing unconsciously? KPCT, January 2005. http://www.clickertraining.com/node/101.

Karen Pryor. The shape of shaping: Some historical notes. KPCT, April 2007. http://www.clickertraining.com/node/1135.

Karen Pryor. The eight ways of changing behavior. KPCT, September 2012. http://www.clickertraining.com/node/290.

Karla Jo Helms. Cybercrime statistics expose five industries most susceptible to phishing attacks. PR Newswire, May 2011. http://www.prnewswire.com/news-releases/cybercrime-statistics-expose-five-industries-most-susceptible-to-phishing-attacks-122436438.html.

Melanie Greenberg. Nine essential qualities of mindfulness. Psychology Today, February 2012. https://www.psychologytoday.com/blog/the-mindful-self-express/201202/nine-essential-qualities-mindfulness.

© Jordan Schroeder 2017

J. Schroeder, *Advanced Persistent Training*, DOI 10.1007/978-1-4842-2835-7

Nancy Toppel; Allen Smith. Use of spear phishing exercises to increase security awareness. Proceedings of the 14th Colloquium for Information Systems Security Education, June 2010. http://cisse.info/resources/archives/category/14-papers?download=165:1716-2010.

NRC. The problem of changing food habits. Bulletin of the National Research Council, (108):35–65, October 1943.

Oliver Rochford. Security awareness training: It's the psychology, stupid! SecurityWeek, September 2012. http://www.securityweek.com/security-awareness-training-its-psychology-stupid.

Ponemon. The state of information security awareness: Trends and developments. Technical report, Ponemon Institute, 2014. https://www.securityinnovation.com/uploads/pci-ponemon-whitepaper.pdf.

Ponnurangam Kumaraguru; Justin Cranshaw; Alessandro Acquisti; Lorrie Cranor; Jason Hong; Mary Ann Blair; Theodore Pham. School of phish: A real-world evaluation of anti-phishing training. Carnegie Mellon University, June 2009. http://cups.cs.cmu.edu/soups/2009/proceedings/a3-kumaraguru.pdf.

Ponnurangam Kumaraguru; Yong Rhee; Steve Sheng; Sharique Hasan; Alessandro Acquisti; Lorrie Cranor; Jason Hong. Getting users to pay attention to anti-phishing education: Evaluation of retention and transfer. Technical report, Carnegie Mellon University, 2007.

Richard Fry. This year, millennials will overtake baby boomers. Pew Research Center, January 2015. http://www.pewresearch.org/fact-tank/2015/01/16/this-year-millennials-will-overtake-baby-boomers/.

SANS. 2015 security awareness report. Technical report, SANS Securing The Human, 2015. http://www.securingthehuman.org/media/resources/STH-SecurityAwarenessReport-2015.pdf.

Samantha Manke; Ira Winkler. The habits of highly successful security awareness programs: A cross-company comparison. Technical report, Secure Mentem, 2012. http://www.securementem.com/wp-content/uploads/2013/07/Habits_white_paper.pdf.

Sean Gallagher. DHS infosec chief: We should pull clearance of feds who fail phish test. Ars Technica, September 2015a. http://arstechnica.com/security/2015/09/dhs-infosec-chief-we-should-pull-clearance-of-feds-who-fail-phish-test/.

Steve Corbett. Targeting different generations. Encyclopedia of Educational Technology, 2008. http://www.stevecorbett.net/edtecportfolio/generations/start.htm.

Taylor Armerding. Millennials becoming known as Generation Leaky. CSO
    Online, February 2015. http://www.csoonline.com/article/2884638/
    security-awareness/millennials-becoming-known-as-generation-
    leaky.html.

Thanuja Vasudevan. Cyber goons phish beyond financial transactions. Financial
    Chronicle, August 2010.

Tim Greene. Phishing scams dupe the most active online users. Network World,
    April 2011. http://www.networkworld.com/article/2201901/malware-
    cybercrime/phishing-scams-dupe-the-most-active-online-users.html.

William Jackson. To defeat phishing, energy learns to phish. GCN, June 2011.
    https://gcn.com/articles/2011/06/13/doe-phishing-test.aspx.

Index

© Jordan Schroeder 2017
J. Schroeder, *Advanced Persistent Training*, DOI 10.1007/978-1-4842-2835-7

Get the eBook for only $5!

Why limit yourself?

With most of our titles available in both PDF and ePUB format, you can access your content wherever and however you wish—on your PC, phone, tablet, or reader.

Since you've purchased this print book, we are happy to offer you the eBook for just $5.

To learn more, go to http://www.apress.com/companion or contact support@apress.com.

Apress®

Printed in the United States
By Bookmasters